A Sketch of the Life of Okah Tubbee

(Called) William Chubbee, Son of the Head Chief, Mo-sholeh Tubbee, of the Choctaw Nation of Indians

W0018001

By Laah Ceil Manatoi Elaah Tubbee

A DocSouth Books Edition
The University of North Carolina at Chapel Hill Library
Chapel Hill

A DocSouth Books Edition, 2018

ISBN 978-1-4696-4178-2(pbk.: alk. paper)

Published by
The University of North Carolina at Chapel Hill Library
CB #3900 Davis Library
Chapel Hill, NC 27514-8890
http://library.unc.edu

Documenting the American South
http://docsouth.unc.edu
docsouth@unc.edu

Distributed by
The University of North Carolina Press
116 South Boundary Street
Chapel Hill, NC 27514-3808
1-800-848-6224
http://www.uncpress.org

This book was digitally printed.

About This Edition

This edition is made available under the imprint of DocSouth Books, a collaborative endeavor between the University of North Carolina at Chapel Hill Library and the University of North Carolina Press. Titles in DocSouth Books are drawn from the Library's Documenting the American South (DocSouth) digital publishing program, online at docsouth.unc.edu. These print and downloadable e-book editions have been prepared from the DocSouth electronic editions.

Both DocSouth and DocSouth Books present the transcribed content of historic books as they were originally published. Grammar, punctuation, spelling, and typographical errors are therefore preserved from the original editions. DocSouth Books are not intended to be facsimile editions, however. Details of typography and page layout in the original works have not been preserved in the transcription.

DocSouth Books editions incorporate two pagination schemas. First, standard page numbers reflecting the pagination of this edition appear at the top of each page for easy reference. Second, page numbers in brackets within the text (e.g., "[Page 9]") refer to the pagination of the original publication; online versions of the DocSouth works use this same original pagination. Page numbers shown in tables of contents and book indexes, when present, refer to the original works' printed page numbers and therefore correspond to the page numbers in brackets.

Summary

Historical records indicate that Okah Tubbee, originally known as Warner McCary, was born in Natchez, Mississippi, around 1810 to an enslaved African American woman known as Franky. Tubbee later denied that she was his real mother. When Franky's master, James McCary, died in 1813, his will freed Franky and her two older children (possibly McCary's offspring), but directed that Tubbee and his offspring "be held as slaves during all and each of their lives" (Littlefield p. ix). Tubbee's true lineage remains unknown, but scholars have questioned his self-asserted Native American ancestry. It is also unclear when Warner McCary began to use the name Okah Tubbee, but as a young man, he went by various names, including James Warner, William McCary, and simply Cary. In 1836, he left Natchez by riverboat, and from 1837 to 1840 he worked at Leeds Foundry in New Orleans, with intermittent stints as a musician and cigar vendor along the Mississippi and Ohio Rivers. During this period, he met and married Laah Ceil, the daughter of a Delaware Indian mother and a Mohawk (or Mahican) father. In 1843, aided by local whites who believed him to be a Native American, Warner McCary received a permit to reside in Mississippi as a free person of color. In 1844 he left Mississippi, and over the next several years he performed as a musician and lecturer in Missouri, Illinois, Indiana, Iowa, Ohio, Kentucky, Virginia, Maryland, and Washington, D.C. By 1847, Tubbee was widely known as an Indian doctor and the son of a Choctaw chief (p. xx). Tubbee's legend grew along with his fame, and by 1849 he was reportedly able to speak 14 different languages and play over 50 musical instruments (p. xxviii). Over the next several years, Tubbee and his family were hounded by debts, malpractice lawsuits, and threats and were repeatedly forced to relocate. In 1852, they settled in Toronto, Canada, where Tubbee established a quiet medical practice and continued to speak on behalf of Native American interests. In 1854, Tubbee was targeted by a medical reform movement, and the Toronto Globe derided him as an "Indian quack doctor" (p. xxxv). Tubbee's biographies end with his brief period of prosperity, and the details of his subsequent life and death—as well as the fates of his family members—remain unknown.

Laah Ceil was born in New York in 1817; her family moved to Missouri following an 1818 treaty in which the Delaware Indians agreed to relocate to the James Fork of the White River. A subsequent treaty required them to move again to a territory near the Kansas-Missouri border, and she met Warner McCary a/k/a Okah Tubbee soon afterwards (Littlefield p. xxv). Encouraged by Reverend Lewis Allen, a published author and traveling lecturer for the temperance movement, Laah Ceil recorded a narrative of her husband's life in 1848, and Allen added an introductory essay. The original publication of A Thrilling Sketch of the Life of the Distinguished Chief Okah Tubbee mistakenly listed Allen as the sole author, giving no credit to Laah Ceil, but a revised version appeared later that year, clearly attributed to "Laah Ceil Manatoi Elaah Tubbee, His Wife," and a Toronto publisher published this expanded version in 1852.

After two testimonials from friends who vouch for Okah Tubbee's flute-playing abilities and a program from a performance introduced by Laah Ceil (and featuring an appearance by their two-year-old son Bruce), the 1852 Sketch includes a lightly edited version of Lewis Allen's "Essay Upon the Indian Character" from the original publication. It also reprints the so-called Indian Covenant "between the Six Nations and the Choctaws," signed by "Pochongehala" (p. 14). The narrative begins with brief recollections of his father and Tubbee's childhood with his "unnatural mother." Tubbee then recounts an incident in which a group of bears approaches and inspects but does not harm him (p. 17).

Most of the content in the 1852 Sketch is close or identical to the 1848 Thrilling Sketch, although certain portions are rearranged or expanded. For example, in the later text, Tubbee's visit to the Choctaw Indians in Alexandria is described before his apprenticeship to the cruel blacksmith Mr. Russell (pp. 26-33). The later version also includes a significant new passage about Tubbee's apprenticeship to Dr. A.P. Merrill, demonstrating his interest in medicine, his practical training, and his desire to become an "Indian Doctor" (p. 22). Admitting his inability to read, Tubbee recalls his informal education as a process of trial and error: "eagerly I watched each symptom, the progress of the disease, and if arrested by my simple medicine, I carefully noted each change, thereby instructing myself, often acknowledging that practice makes perfect" (p. 23).

In addition, the 1852 version expands Tubbee's account of his travels, first as a musician with the Louisiana Volunteers and later on his own. During one trip, he rides a series of steamboats up the Ohio River to Lake Erie, visiting Cincinnati, Cleveland, Pittsburgh, and Detroit (p. 48). He also relates his journey to Florida to visit the Creek and Seminole Indians, where, not surprisingly, his message that whites "would never give up the chase until the Indian was no longer an inhabitant of that soil" was unwelcome (p. 50). During this journey, which the earlier biography does not mention, an old acquaintance of the Choctaw chief Mosholeh Tubbee identifies Okah Tubbee as the chief's son, and another of Mosholeh Tubbee's sons recognizes Okah Tubbee "like brothers" (pp. 54, 69).

Towards the end of his narrative, Tubbee expresses a desire to let his wife, Laah Ceil, "speak for herself, for she does not like to hear me say that we made an engagement the first day, made an acquaintance the next, and was married so soon" (pp. 74-75). In this final, additional section, Laah Ceil describes her birth, her education, her Christian convictions, and the manner in which she met and married Tubbee. She also recounts their travels together and their advocacy "in behalf of the Indians" and against forced relocation (p. 79). The 1852 *Sketch* concludes with an original poem by Laah Ceil and a collection of letters, documents, and vouchers attesting to Okah Tubbee's identity and his medical skill.

Works Consulted

Brennan, Jonathan, ed., *Mixed Race Literature*, Stanford: Stanford University Press, 2002; Brennan, Jonathan, "African-Native American Literature," *Africana: The Encyclopedia of the African and African American Experience*, 2nd ed., Kwame Anthony Appiah and Henry Louis Gates, Jr., eds., available through Oxford African American Studies Center online ; Gilmore, Paul, *The Genuine Article: Race, Mass Culture, and American Literary Manhood*, Durham: Duke University Press, 2001; Littlefield, Daniel F., Jr., Introduction, *The Life of Okah Tubbee*, Lincoln: U of Nebraska P, 1988.

Patrick E. Horn

*Assisted by Mrs. LAAH CEIL TUBBEE a descendant of
the Mohawk Tribe, C. W.*

OKAH, in presenting to the public the following Testimonials from his kind friends, Madame ANNA BISHOP and Mr. BOCHSA, presumes they will be sufficient vouchers for his ability:

DEAR SIR,—Your friend, OKAH TUBBEE, plays on the Flute most exquisitely; he evinces great musical taste, and deserves well to with success.

I am, dear sir, yours, &c.

ANNA BISHOP.

BUFFALO, 29th July, 1851.

DEAR SIR,—

BUFFALO, August 1st, 1851

I have great pleasure in expressing to you my satisfaction respecting the abilities of OKAH TUBBEE. He is, indeed, a very remarkable person, and performs on the Flute admirably; it is astonishing that with a common wooden instrument, not possessing any additional keys, OKAH TUBBEE can play so well in tune, and have such a powerful tone. His variations on simple subjects are clever and neatly done, and no doubt he will succeed well.

Believe me, dear sir, yours truly,

CH. BOCHSA.

On this occasion he will perform some of his most extraordinary and popular pieces on his One-keyed

Flute; Sauce Panana; Musical Tomahawk; Flageolet; Fife, with three fingers of one

hand, accompanying himself with Castinets with the other hand.
THEY WILL APPEAR
IN THEIR RICH AND MUCH ADMIRED INDIAN COSTUME.

PART FIRST.

The Evening's Entertainment will commence with a short
   Address by Mrs. Laah Ceil Tubbee,
      Giving an Interesting Account of her People.
After which the Chief will introduce their YOUNG BRUCE, 2 years of
   age, in full costume of the Brave.
   1.—Life in New York, his own much admired variations, on the Musical Walking Stick.
   2.—Auld Lang Syne, Flute, unequalled variations arranged by himself.
   3—Lauden's Boney Woods and Braes—Flute variations.
   4.—Killey Cranky—Flageolette, by placing it in the nostril.
   5.—*Bruce's Address to his Army—Flute, also arranged by himself.*

AN INTERMISSION OF TEN MINUTES.

PART SECOND.

   1.—Life let us cherish—Musical Walking Stick.
   2.—Lord Hornbrook's Grand March.
   3.—Aurora Waltz—Flute, in a new and much admired.
   4.—Kinlock to Kinlock—his own beautiful .
   5.—Okah Tubbee's own Waltz—Flute, composed by himself.
   6.—*Marseilles Hymn—Walking-cane, in his own peculiar style.*

In offering this Entertainment to the Public, he hopes to give such a variety as will not fail to meet the approbation of all classes of the community; and in so doing, good order must be observed, as the performer depends upon his exertions to please, and by his respectability of person and performance to share the patronage of a generous public.

Doors open at half-past 7,—Performance to commence at 8. Admittance ls. 10½d. Children, ls.

A SKETCH OF THE LIFE
OF
OKAH TUBBEE,
(CALLED)
WILLIAM CHUBBEE,
SON OF THE HEAD CHIEF,
MOSHOLEH TUBBEE, OF THE
CHOCTAW NATION OF INDIANS.

BY

LAAH CEIL MANATOI ELAAH TUBBEE, HIS WIFE.

TORONTO:
PRINTED FOR OKAH TUBBEE,
BY HENRY STEPHENS.
1852.

[Page 3] *INDIAN CHARACTER.*

IN contemplating the Indian character, there is an interest thrown around it, which cannot fail to impress the mind of every inquiring person. Although the Indian race is fading away, their palmy days being gone, yet their is a charm thrown around their past history, and the most lively emotions are created in the mind of the patriot and philanthropist in contemplating their past and present history; and we are led to look upon the high and lofty bearing of the red man with the most intense admiration. There was a period in the history of the aborigines of North America, when they reigned as supreme lords over this vast continent. The Yonkoo tribe, which means literally conqueror, had undisputed away over the New England country. The term Yankee comes from the tribe of Indians styled Yonkoo. The English conquered them after a long and bloody contest; when blood had flown in crimson currents, and the shrieks of many an innocent and massacred female rent the air, and the red man's tomahawk was wreaking in the blood of its victim; and when they were subdued, the war chief, a proud and noble fellow stepped forth, and presented his tomahawk to the officer in command of the English forces, saying, "Me yonkoo," or conqueror, "but now you yonkoo." Hence the term has been twisted about until it has become Yankee.

The English named the six States, New Hampshire, Massachusetts, Connecticut, Rhode Island, Vermont, and Maine, New England, in contradistinction to Old England. We Americans call the New Englanders Yankees. Odium sometimes is attached to the term, Yankee, yet candid and unprejudiced minds are willing to admit that the Yankees are a thorough and persevering people. The Massachusetts tribe, inhabited what is now called the State of Massachusetts, the name being derived from the tribes, as are the names of many of the States and Territories. All [Page 4] Indian names are very significant. Take a few merely for the sake of illustration. Tubbee, means Big Chief, not only referring to a great and enlarged mind, but to a powerful tribe, as Chief of the Choctaw nation. Mississippi means father; hence the Mississippi is called the father of waters. How significant!—one of the largest rivers upon the face of the globe, taking its rise in the Rocky mountains, continuing through an immense valley, widening and deepening in its onward course, bearing on its broad bosom a world of commerce, wealth and enterprise, with six thousand trading and two thousand steamboats, moistening and fertilizing the soil of three Territories and ten States, until it pours its mighty waters into the Gulf of Mexico.

It is difficult to arrive at a correct conclusion as to the origin of the Indian race; it is supposed by historians, sacred and profane, ancient and modern, that all the races which have been and now are upon the earth, are derived from Noah; that from Shem, Ham, and Japheth, sprang white, red, and black men, and from them the great variety of nations, kindreds and tongues. Some suppose that the Indians are descended from some of the tribes of Israel; that they pursued a northern course as far as Bherings Straights, and constructed some kind of floating raft, and crossed over where it is only about nineteen miles to one island, and nineteen to another, and took possession of the country before it was discovered by Americus Vespucius or Christopher Columbus. Indeed there is a strong evidence to support this view from tradition, and a similarity of features, &c, There is another fact worthy of consideration. The great number of mounds and tumuli, found in various parts of the United States and Mexico, and Central America, give evidence of their having been constructed by a race in possession of the arts and sciences. Whatever position the Indian may have occupied in past ages, one fact we must admit; that they were the rightful owners of the soil, since Transatlantics found them here, roaming unmolested over these vast domains. They then dwelt secure in their own leafy bowers; they smoked their pipes in their own wigwams, the young Indians chased the wild deer, and skimmed the light canoes over the murmuring streams and silvery lakes; the young Indian girls entwined the wreath around their raven tresses, as beautiful as their own lovely forms. But they have melted away, driven from their own lovely bowers. Nation after nation, and tribe after tribe have passed away. Philip, Logan, Blackhawk, Powhatan, Keokuck, and other noble warriors, have bowed themselves[Page 5] under the crushing weight of misfortunes; disease has spread a pestilence through the tribes; war has swept like a desolating ravager through their lands, and fire-water, like a hydra monster, has swept on its fiery course, carrying its millions to the grave. What a melancholy picture is presented in bold relief to the mind of the philanthropist. How scenes of the most thrilling interest come looming upon the vision. Behold a mother bidding a final farewell to the place of her nativity, to the spot where the light of heaven first fell upon her infant eyes! what tender emotions rush upon her memory! scenes of other days cluster around her, and that which is the most endearing, the tombs of her ancestors. View her standing upon the last green hill pressing her little one to her bosom, covering its little face with her burning tears; she moves on a few steps, and then for the last time bids her long and much loved home farewell forever; often in her migrations to the far west, do scenes of the past crowd upon her memory. At last, with a little remnant of a tribe, they arrive at the place of their new home, and finally, broken-hearted, they sink into the tomb. The white man often in his undue thirst for more land, and want of reflection, ploughs up the very bones of their children, and scatters them to the four winds of heaven. But I will not pursue this painful subject.

There are features in the Indian character to which we invite your attention. An Indian never forgets an injury nor an act of kindness. There are instances on record where Indians have cherished for years feelings of revenge, and have finally avenged the injury. An Indian once in a fit of anger committed murder, and gave himself up immediately, but asked for time to enable him to raise corn, and provide venison for his family, which was allowed him; at the end of six months he came and told the friends of the person whose friend he had killed, that he had provided for his family, and as he had broken the laws of the Great Spirit, and of his nation, he must suffer the penalty and he was ready to die. The brother of the wife of the deceased arose, and deliberately clove his skull through with his tomahawk. They often return good for evil. An instance is related where an Indian applied to a white man for food and shelter, as he had been hunting all day and killed no game, and he was very hungry and tired, but the white man in an angry tone bid the Indian dog be gone. Sometime after this, the white man went out on a hunting excursion, but after hunting all day, was unsuccessful, and losing his way, being weary [Page 6] and hungry, he was about to give up in despair, but seeing the smoke of a wigwam, he hastened to it, but what was his surprise when entering the lodge to find the very Indian he had driven away hungry from his own lodge. He expected immediate death, but the Indian bid welcome, with the utmost kindness, and his squaw prepared him food; be ate and drank, and then he laid down and slept free from all harm. In the morning the Indian gave him his gun, and accompanied him on his journey. Arriving near the white settlement, and pointing through the wood said, "There is the white man's home. You remember poor Indian hungry and tired, ask you give some food, and lie down and sleep in your wigwam; you say no, be gone you Indian—you come by and by to Indian lodge, you tired and hungry, you think Indian kill you, but no, Indian say no, you have wife and children who love you, me look on my squaw and papoose, me love 'em too, me say me no kill white man, and make sorrow and sadness come to his house—you are free, go white man, go to your home, make your wife and children happy, and don't forget poor Indian, how much he suffer, how the white man wronged him."

I remember an instance which occurred in the days of my childhood, which is fresh in my memory. An Indian woman came to the house of my parents, and being very sick asked permission to remain a few days, which was cheerfully granted. On recovering, she left us, returning her thanks. Some months after she returned, bringing with her a number of beautiful baskets which she had made with her own hands, and a quantity of home-made sugar, which she gave to my mother—my mother went to pay her an equivalent, which the Indian woman positively refused, saying, "me sick squaw, you good to squaw, me never forget good squaw for her kindness to poor Indian squaw."

THE RELIGIOUS CHARACTER OF THE INDIANS is very interesting. They universally believe in the existence of God, or the Great Spirit. They greatly venerate him. They feel that his great power has made all things, and that he is every where present, and sees all they do. They never profane the name or character of the Great Spirit. The Indian languages have no terms by which they can profane the Great Spirit. But alas, they have learned it in the English tongue. As also they have learned from the pale face the direful use of the fire-water, as they term whiskey, which is destroying thousands.

The Indians feel and believe that once they were in favour with the Great Spirit, that he loved them, but now he frowns upon them. And [Page 7] that they are subject to the influences of the evil or bad Spirit, to which they sometimes make offerings in order to propitiate him, so that he may not torment them. The Indians also believe in a state of rewards and punishments,—that those who do well among them, when they die will be received by the Great Spirit to a beautiful country where pure rivers flow, and lofty mountains rise, and extended hunting grounds present an abundance of every variety of game, and where the evil Spirit comes not, nor sickness nor death, nor any other affliction. But where there is complete happiness. They believe that those who do evil, or are bad men, will go to a country of an opposite character. A land of dreariness, and of chills. It will be situated in sight of the beautiful and happy country, but those in the bad country can never go to the good one, but must pine away in wretchedness and endless want. They have no knowledge of the Saviour until it is presented to them by the gospel, hence they know nothing of a way of pardon. Still oppressed by a sense of their sins, they are accustomed to make an offering of the first fruits of their grounds every year.

The following view of the present condition of the Choctaw Indians, written in 1846, by a highly respected and devoted Missionary, and teacher at Fort Coffee Academy, Iowa Territory, REV. W. G. MONTGOMERY, *will show that the Indian is not the degraded being that some would have him be, but that he has been endowed with a mind as susceptible of improvement as the pale face.*The Choctaws have a pleasant, and on many considerations, an interesting country, lying between latitude 32 deg. and 35 deg. north. On the north, it is bounded by the Arkansas river, it being the line between them and the Cherokees; on the south the Red River separates them from the State of Texas, on the east they are bounded by the State of Arkansas, on the west by the Creek and Seminole Indians. They have perhaps more territory than half the State of Kentucky. Some portions are very fertile, especially the bottom and low lands on the rivers and creeks. There are a good many extensive praires, some of them are rich, others are too sandy to be productive. On the low lands there are extensive cane brakes and a bottom grass, which keeps green through the winter.

The Porto, Cliamahu and Canadian rivers, with many other smaller rivers and creeks, are all tributaries of the Red River, and Arkansas, [Page 8] and take their rise in, and flow their whole length through the Choctaw country. Steam boats go up the Arkansas River more than a thousand miles, passing several hundred miles into the Indian country. There is a high water in this river always in the months of June and July. There is much mineral wealth from ore, stone, coal, and salt springs, in their country.

THE CLIMATE.—The winters are mild, the summers are very warm, and frequently dry. Cotton and corn grow here in abundance. That migratory disposition so characteristic of the Indian tribes, has in a great measure left the Choctaws, and they wish to be stationary. They do not wish to remove to any other country—they are now improving their lands, building houses, and planting vineyards. Many of these farmers have from ten, twenty, fifty, to one hundred acres in corn, and large fields of cotton. There are few, comparitively speaking, who live by hunting. The buffalo are gone, there are bear and deer, and many other kinds of wild game. During the winter season the whole creation seems alive with the various tribes of birds; the forests and prairies are made to resound with the melody of their notes, and the river and ponds and lakes, are covered with water fowls of various kinds; cattle, horses and hogs are raised in great abundance. He says, "I saw very few sheep among them. It is not uncommon for an Indian man to have five or six hundred head of cattle; I frequently saw from fifty to one hundred and fifty milch cows belonging to one man, the cows and calves are kept gentle by the following course; the calves are put into a pen or lot of an acre or more on the edge of a prairie and are kept in there during the day, and at night the cows are put into the same pen, the calves are turned out into the prairie, where they feed around during the night, and in the morning they are about the fence waiting to be let into the pen with the cows; in the fall they are branded and turned out and live during the winter upon the cane rushes and prairie grass. The horses and cattle are smaller than ours, their horses being most generally of the pony stock.

Christianity has done much for this people, and is still doing more; they may be said to be redeemed from heathenism, and placed upon the high and elevated ground of civilization, the arts and sciences being cultivated by them to some considerable extent. They have a well drawn up and printed Constitution; republican in its character; the elective franchise it committed to the people; the members of the Council are elected every year; crimes are punished by fines and otherwise; [Page 9] the murderer is shot by an officer called the Lighthorseman. There are Washingtonian Temperance Societies among them, and the Temperance cause has many advocates. The tribe may be said to be temperate. The white man is prohibited by law from selling whiskey among them. The new Testament is translated into their language, and many other little historical and religious tracts, hymn books, &c. &c. And now the weapons of war are beaten into ploughshares, and no longer is the war whoop heard, but songs of Zion may be heard from their cabins and houses, and places of worship are built for the true and living God. Oh! for the salvation of God to all the aborigines of the wilderness. By an act of their Council, they have set apart forever, more than six hundred thousand dollars, of their annuity money as a fund, the interest of which is to be appropriated to educational purposes. There are three National Academies now established among them, where twenty thousand dollars are expended annually for the education of their youth. The Fort Coffee Academy is located on the Arkansas River, and is under the control of the M. E. C. S. The Spencer Academy is within a few miles of Red River, and-under the control of the Presbyterian Church, Old School. The Armstrong Academy on Chiamechia river, is under the control of the Baptist Church. The children who enter these Academies are selected by the Trustees, two from each Indian family, some of them come one hundred and fifty miles without names, in their Indian costume. They are expected to remain four years, during which time they complete the following English branches of education; reading, writing, arithmetic, grammar and geography, and learn to talk the English language. The senior class then enters upon the study of the ancient languages and the higher branches of the English. After going through a preparatory course, some members of this class will be sent to the best colleges and universities in the United States, where they will remain until they graduate. Each of the aforesaid Academies is expected to take under its care one hundred students, where they are clothed, boarded and instructed. The buildings for the female department at Fort Coffee are frame, and were put up at an expense of three thousand dollars. The boys are taught agriculture. They spend three hours a day on the farm at work; the girls are instructed in sewing, knitting, and the science of housewifery; these Academies are all on the manual labour system. There are several other missionary schools among them, (the Choctaws) [Page 10] supported entirely by the money of the Missionary Societies, and there are now, at least five hundred of their children going to their schools and academies now in successful operation among them. Workshops are intended to be established with each of the three National Academies, and a part of each day spent in learning the different trades of mechanism. The population of this tribe is about thirty thousand.

[Page 11] *INDIAN COVENANT.*

The following account given me a few years since in the Indian Territory by Pochongehala the son of the grandfather of the Six Nations, may serve to show how the Indians settle difficulties among themselves. It is a sketch of the Covenant and the ratifying of it made and entered into by and between the Six Nations and the Choctaws, and of their united effort to bring the Osages into it. Indeed, it was the commencement of a plan, originated entirely with the Indians, to effect a universal peace among themselves.

When the Covenant was presented by the Six Nations to Mosholeh Tubbee and McIntosh, chiefs of the Choctaw Nations, it was readily received and an agreement formed between them. Then the wise men (or chiefs,) of the Choctaws and Six Nations went over the river to propose it to the Osages, and they would not treat with them, but offered to call the young men together, and all that might be wishing to take the Covenant. They then left them and returned to the Choctaw Nation, as the Six Nations had not finished their road* any farther; they left the Covenant with the Choctaws, and told them they would return in a few days.** They left them the word, also the token, which was wampum.***

In a few days they returned back to the Choctaws, and together went to treat with the Osages, sending six men before them (to the Osage Nation,) to remind them of the talk. Some of them were of the Six Nations, some Choctaws. Chief Tubbee was one. When they came near, knowing them to be warlike, they sent in a part of their men, the Osages said, in so many suns setting, and so many suns rising, their Chiefs and young men would be ready to meet them in Council. Agreeable [Page 12] to the request of the Osages they returned, and found the Osages prepared for defence, with a kind of brush fort, ditched about inside and outside, piqueted with brush

---

* Meaning *plan.*

** Used to signify an indefinite period.

*** The *Wampum* is a symbolical representation worked in beads or painted; used by the Indians to express their wishes or ideas.

and poles. They wished to get the Osages word, and would not be repulsed by their warlike appearance. Their word was, that they would not all receive their Covenant, yet some of them had been weak enough to do so, and had hung the tokens in their ears. They are your men, but we are not, but choose to stand by ourselves. The Choctaws and Six Nations were friends, their errand was peace, and they asked, will you receive our Covenant? The Osages were very independent, and said they would not willingly, but told them as they were their grandfathers, they must make them do so, as children had sometimes to be whipped into obedience. The Chiefs that were treating with them, bade them to recollect that their grandfather was like a *Bear;* whenever he laid his toe-nail down, he was always sure to gain the ground. They told him they would come back in a few days in peace, as they should now return to the Choctaws, and when they returned to them again, if they received not the peace, they would cause them to do so by chastisement. They likewise so did. After they were whipped, they wandered between the two rivers, supposed to be the Mississippi and Missouri, but their grandfather followed them there, and then made them receive the Covenant of Peace. The Chiefs of the Six Nations were not willing to leave the Covenant with them, although they had made their road thus far, and the emblems thereof were worked on the Wampum, but chose to carry it back and leave it with the Choctaws, called in their original tongue, *Oyataw,* signifying a large Nation. The Mississippi River, they called Oyatawgah, because of its size, and having many snags. Now this people was called by them Oyataw. The Cherokee Nation claimed to be the same who treated with the Six Nations at this time, but the grandfather says it was the Choctaw, and that they knew no difference then between the Cherokees and Choctaws; but finding them all living on this great river, named them after it, as one great nation, the Oyataw. But they found the Choctaws many days afterwards, acknowledging the same men to have been their Chiefs. Furthermore, let the Council be examined; here we find the Cherokees have not got the Covenant of Peace left by the Chiefs of the North or Six Nations; neither the speeches, significations, or articles belonging thereunto, except a very few, neither do they explain or seem to know the use of these illustrations. Thus we are left to judge that they never really belonged to that portion of the [Page 13] Oyataw but they have been separated away by their Chiefs and called Cherokees. But the Six Nations knew them in these days the Oyataw, *One Nation.* Furthermore, this has not been extended any farther in a proper manner, or any thing done as should have been, though the Chiefs have made many trials; except one Covenant of Peace made by George Herron, with the Camanches. This was rightly done, the only one that has been conducted after the pattern since the Six Nations and the Oyataw covenanted together with the Osages. Furthermore, let the old men of the Six Nations treat the Choctaw and Cherokee as seemeth them good; receive them as two nations, search out their chiefs, wise men, their fathers, and their families, and let them be received in order in the Covenant, or else consider them as one, the former Oyataw, and let the Six Nations ascertain and point out those of the families of their former Chiefs, namely, Tubbee, the McIntosh, that the braves of the Choctaws need no longer say, as they said to me in the Cherokee Council. "We have no head, no elderly wise men; the Tubbee is gone; his family, none of them survive him to our knowledge. We are babes in the sayings of our fathers, and request our grandfather of the Six Nations to teach us." I asked them for the Pipe of Peace given them by the Chiefs of the Six Nations, and described it by saying it was one half white and one half red. It could not at first be found. I thought this might throw some light on the gloom that darkened the hopes—even the dying request of the loved, the brave, the lamented Big Chief or Tubbee of the Oyataw Nation, respecting the youngest son of his, who was with the pale face. Furthermore, many evil designing men, have reported that this child was dead; others that Chief Tubbee had no such child, and now had no heir living. Others said there was such a person, but that his origin had never been traced out, and many disputed his being the son of their Chief. These statements were made at the last Council, when the Choctaws said if they could find him, they would serve him and love him. At length the Pipe was brought, having been found, among the Cherokees; the grandfather knew that it was left with Tubbee. The pipe was injured; the articles of the Covenant scattered among the two divisions. The braves understood not the talk of their grandfather. But their silent and confused faces showed they were children in the affairs of their nation, and they again requested to be taught; but the grandfather being grieved at heart, determined to seek out the lost one—the child of their worthy Chief, and divert his mind from his pale faced friends to his own people, if possible. He has [Page 14] succeeded; he is proud and satisfied; thankful to the Great Spirit, that so fine a mind, so much national talent, upright principle, is concentrated in the son, the representative of the long distinguished line of noble Chiefs, the Tubbees. Grateful respects to the pale face friends for their care and attention to the grandfather, whose heart is warm, being pleased with his prize, as he bears a strong personal resemblance to his father, only the father was taller and heavier built. Now may the pale face and the red man dwell peacefully together, is the desire and prayer of the grandfather.

Respectfully,

POCHONGEHALA.

[Page 15] NARRATIVE.

SKETCH OF THE EVENTFUL LIFE OF OKAH TUBBEE, (CALLED) WILLIAM CHUBBEE.

[Here commences a true narrative, drawn up from his own lips.]

FIRST RECOLLECTIONS.

THE first recollections of my childhood are scenes of sorrow; though I have an imperfect recollection of a kind father, who was a very large man, with dark red skin, and his head was adorned with feathers of a most beautiful plumage. I seem to have been happy then, and remember the green woods, and that he took me out at night, and taught me to look up to the stars, and said many things to me that made my young heart swell with sweet hope, as it filled with thoughts too large for it to retain. This scene soon changed, for I had a new father, or a man who took me to a new home, which proves to have been Natchez, Mississippi. I have no recollection where this intercourse took place with my own father, but from various circumstances which have since occured, I am led to believe that it must have been upon the Dancing Rabbit Creek, (Tombigbee) before the Choctaws removed from their old homes. I soon found this was not my own father, neither in appearance nor in action, and began to understand that I could have but one father. This man was white, and a slave woman had the management of his house, she had two children, who were older than myself, a boy and a girl; she was very fond of them, but was never even kind to me, yet they obliged me to call her mother. I was always made to serve the two children, [Page 16] though many times I had to be whipped into obedience. If I had permission to go out an hour to play, I choose to be alone, that I might weep over my situation; but even this consolation was refused me. I was forced to go in company with them, taking with me, many times, a smarting back, after a promise had been extorted from me that I would remain with them and obey them. I soon found myself boxing heartily with the boys, both white and black, because they called me an ill name, and every thing but that which was true, for I could not and would not submit to such gross insults without defending myself, which is so characteristic of the red man. Her children were well dressed and neat; I was not only in rags, but many times my proud heart seemed crushed within me, and my cheek crimsoned with shame because of their filthy condition, and I often left them off in consequence, but soon learned to take them off and wash them myself, such was my abhorence of filth. I was compelled to go in a naked state to enable me to wash my clothes, and they upbraided me for my nakedness, but I replied, where did you ever see or hear of a child being born with clothes on? I was then a child too young to work, but did errands.

NARROW ESCAPE FROM THE BEARS.

Messrs. Spencer Grayson and Joseph B. Davis, (son-in-law of Levi Pernell, who resided in Natchez, on Second North Street, as long ago as I can recollect,) entrusted me with the performance of several duties, which having faithfully executed, and thereby securing their friendship, I gladly learned that Mr. Davis had made successful application for me to accompany him on a visit to his plantation in the back part of the State of Mississippi. This was my first journeying, and Mr. Davis had to tie me upon the horse. Some laughed at the idea of his taking so small a child with him, but nothing could change his mind; he declared that I should have at least a few weeks pleasure. The woman who had the care of me was very angry with me at this time, and told Mr. Davis that she wished she had never seen me, and desired him never to bring me back; but he said, "Never mind, aunty, fortune will take care of him. I expect he will outlive us both." After travelling four or five days, Mr. Davis tried me without fastening me to the saddle. I could now manage my horse very well, and keep up also. About the third day Mr. Davis had grown careless about me, as I took good care of myself and horse, and he found he had lost his way while passing through [Page 17] a cane brake. We wandered around for some time, and at length came to a strip of fence, decayed or thrown down, so that it was scarcely breast high to the horses. Mr. Davis in his hurry had forgotten me, and was thinking only of the road. He did not stop for the fence, so I followed suit, but soon stopped on the ground, the breath beat out of my body, so that I could not call for some time. Mr. Davis was out of sight. I got upon my horse again and rushed on in the course which I thought he had taken. I thought I discovered a small path, into which I reined my horse, but the care was so large and so tall that I could not proceed. I thought that I could go better on foot; so I contrived to get down, and groped my way along the little path. I had not gone far, when I found my path was much wider, but I did not get upon my horse again. I at length heard a noise which I could not understand, but I had heard people talking of wild hogs, and concluded that there were some near, as I could hear them snuffing, and as I thought, the young ones playing. I looked earnestly around, and to my astonishment saw two animals, which I knew must be bears, from the fact of having seen a tame one at Mr. Philip Brill's, at Natchez. The old ones walked up, smelling of me as they came; the young ones playing a little way off. I did not try to run, for I thought it was of no use. I expected they would kill me, but after examining me they turned and walked away, their young ones following them. My path had led me into the big road, and the bears took one way and I the other. I knew by the neighing of my faithful horse, and the answer he received, that I was near Mr. Davis. I hurried on, and soon came up with him, and found him on the banks of a river, standing by his horse. I told him what had passed, and he said that he had gone back to look for me, and happened to get his eye on me just as he saw the bears walk up to me. He embraced me, the tears gushing from his eyes; he said that he feared to try to rescue me, lest he should aggravate the animals, and thereby cause them to tear me in pieces before his eyes; that he in horror turned away, lest he should see me die, and when he heard the horse neigh he did not expect again to see me alive; but said he thought that wicked woman's wish was granted. He stated that it reminded him of his saying that Providence would protect me.

We reached his plantation the next evening in safety; when after finishing his business on his farm, we started towards home together. At Greenville, he was unexpectedly called another way on business. We were within a few days ride of home, when he met an acquaintance, [Page 18] Lawyer Smith, who was going to Natchez, and who offered to see me there. Mr. Davis thought it well that I should go home. I was sorry to part with my friend, but soon had the satisfaction of seeing him in Natchez, and hearing related from his own lips my narrow escape.

FISHING EXCURSIONS.

A very aged man obtained of this unnatural mother leave for me to go with him to Shelling's Lake to fish. He set me holding his line, and showed me how to manage it, and oh, what a proud moment was this to my little heart, and with what ecstacy did I gaze upon the fish as I drew it out of its native element, struggling for life. I was so fortunate as to catch one more fish than the old man; this encouraged me much; a new world sprang up before me. I then began to contrive how I could possess myself of a hook and line. I could imitate many sounds, such as the mewing of a cat, the barking, howling, and growling of a dog, &c. Some gentlemen overhearing me, gave me a few pence. I was so delighted with the money which I received, that I could hardly contain myself; not because I loved money, but because it secured my wishes. I went twice with the old man, after which I went alone and caught twelve or fourteen dozen fishes. I took the money home to this unnatural mother, and asked her to buy me some clothes, for my fish brought me half a dollar a dozen; but she retained the money, and the only satisfaction I had, was to be compelled to follow her and her children to the store, and see her expend it for finery for her daughter, and then to carry it home. I had, however the satisfaction of retaining a trout and perch line, with a hook for each, which I had hid under the pavement, with a few pence; although they were steel, they were more valuable to me than silver or gold. After this little experiment when I wished to enjoy a fishing excursion, I was obliged to run away. I laid up money enough to purchase a suit of clothes; my bank was the brick pavement, my banker was my fish hook and lines, my cashier was my own hands, and my associates my own brains. At length I got a lawyer to obtain me a suit of clothes with my own money, but I not only had the mortification of having them taken from me, but given to her boy, and by way of interest received a sound flogging;

and here I remember hearing her for the first time in her anger, call me an outlandish savage; although I could not understand it, yet it made a peculiar impression on my young mind. At [Page 19] night, when I ought to have been sleeping, I was rolling on my bed, watering my pillow with my tears, thinking of the advice of my old friend, the coloured man, who was a preacher, and truly a good man, who taught me to pray and to hope for better days. When he died, I lost a true friend, and I was almost overwhelmed at the loss.

THE MUNCE FAMILY.

About this time I became acquainted with a family by the name of Munce, who were always very kind to me. The house of Mr. Thomas Munce was kindly offered me as a home, when I was unable to obtain one in any other way. Mrs. Munce often took me upon her lap and consoled me in my grief, and taught me to think of my Heavenly Father, and to pray to him. They were true friends to me to the very last, and I can never express my obligations or thankfulness to them. I have seen them several times since.

FRUITS OF EARLY WHISTLING.

By this time I had become quite a whistler, and by this method, and other means, had obtained quite a sum of money again, and I employed the same lawyer who had assisted me on a former occasion, to purchase me another suit of clothes, and the lawyer went and told the woman that he had presented them to me, and that she must let me wear them. She did so, and I was so thankful for it that I was willing to give her anything which I could make by my ingenuity. She could not bear to hear me praised, especially above her own children, and she forbade my receiving any more presents. I then hired out to doctors and lawyers to sweep their offices, &c. Some were kind enough to feed me and pay me something; others fed me only, and took me home to their families.

CRUEL TREATMENT OF THE COLORED WOMAN IN WHOSE HANDS I HAD BEEN PLACED BY HER MASTER.

I gave the woman my money, also the presents I received, but the more I gave her, the more she exacted from me. Child as I was, I could not allow myself to weep by day. If she found my pillow wet with my tears, she whipped me for that, and I formed a habit of going [Page 20] alone at night, and lifting my heart to God in prayer, for his preservation; and that my father might return. When I stood thus alone, in the open air, a feeling of hope was within my heart, as I felt thus alone before God, with the stars, which, in my childish language, I called the eyes of heaven, gazing down upon me; here I gained fortitude to bear all my wrongs—here I determined to ask the white man, who brought me here, about my own father. I had now and then mentioned it to the woman, she always told with tongue and heart, begone! outlandish savage, you never had any father. As she was always angry at my inclination to be alone about this time, she gave me a severe whipping for climbing a bluff, which no other boy dared to, and thus spending a Sabbath with my thoughts, tears, prayers, and childish aspirations. This point was called Buzzard Roost. I have since thought she in her anger, forgot herself at this time, for she asked me if I did not know that this was the way Indians and all wild savages lived, and could not be tamed; that the white people could not make as much service of them, as they could of the blacks, for they would not work for them, but spent their lives in wandering about in the woods, both day and night, living with the wild beasts. Now I loved wild beasts, and my heart was swelling within me; I forgot her evil blows, as with clasped hands, and tearful eyes, my heart kindled with the most intense emotion at her recital. I cried out, Oh! tell me more, tell me more. she looked at me, said something about the strange wild light in my eyes—seated herself, and seemed in deep thought. She then said something which I did not understand, though I listened, for I thought she was going to tell me more. I think she said in a soliloquy, "what is bred in the bone will be in the marrow," consequently. when I hear the remark, my mind resorts to this scene of my childhood with peculiar emotion and intense interest. I accordingly asked the white man where he found me, and when my father would come for me. He seemed astonished to find I had any recollection of a father before I saw him. He told me I had been dreaming that he was not my father, bade me remember I was this woman's child, and she could do as she pleased with me; bade me never to mention this thing to any one, nor speak of it again to him; but told me that I would know more about it when old enough to work. Here I gave myself up to despair, and run away and went into the back part of the city. I had often been nearly starved, and thought I could stand hunger pretty well, and managed to climb up and sleep in an old [Page 21] hay loft; but I became very hungry and knew not what to do, as I was unacquainted here, and wished to remain in secret lest I should be taken back. My spirits were so much broken that I could not enter into my old pranks to gain me friends. I sat myself down early in the morning, near a fine looking house, thinking what I should do. I could not bear to beg. There chanced to come to feed their dogs, some of the inmates of the house. As soon as their backs were turned, I hastened to the spot, and with all the strength I had, begged the poor dogs for a morsel of food to prevent me from starving. My hunger made it sweet to me. For some time I slept upon my bed of hay at night, and watched the shaking of table-cloths, and with the dogs picked up the crumbs that were thrown from the tables of the owners. I could not endure this kind of life, and began to search for work. I at length hired to assist in a brick kiln. I passed a few weeks here as happy as my feelings would allow, but a woman who knew my pretended mother, recognized me, and gave information. I was taken back. They had searched much for me, also advertized for me. The brick maker had heard of the search, but never supposed that it referred to me. He had often spoken to me of my red skin, saying I resembled Indian boys he had often seen about Natchez. I then had the privilege of asking what Indian savages meant, and received satisfactory answers. They told much of them which excited my curiosity; that brought to my mind scenes of my earliest recollection. They had faded from my mind, yet I determined, if my life was spared, I would visit that people. This unnatural mother, after her old custom, stripped me to give me a lashing; but at the sight of my bruised and lacerated body, she seemed to have some relentings, and I thought was moved for a moment even to pity. The reason of my being thus mangled, was in consequence of refusing to return. They beat me and lashed me so unmercifully with a cowhide, that my body was black and blue. She then said she wished she had never seen me or the man who had brought me there. She seemed to have given up all hopes of conquering me, and said she ought to tell all she knew and get rid of me, lest I should do something in my fits of anger of an awful nature. She then bade me put on my clothes and begone out of her sight, and told me to remember that at some future time she should punish me. I then went to Major Young of the U. S. Army, who was then stationed there, and through his influence I obtained a situation with a Physician, Dr. A. P. Merrill, who was also a Surgeon in the U. S. Army.

[Page 22]While residing with this kind friend, it was often my place to show the applicant to the Physician. I soon began to read physiognomy, I became accustomed to the faltering step and pallid cheek of those who sought medical treatment for their own infirmities. When opportunity afforded. I listened attentively to the recital of their sufferings, and marked each word or gesture of the Physician. Now and then the aged man came, a dear child or perhaps companion must be seen quickly; I marked the anxiety that seemed to light up his care-worn features—saddened as it were, by a shade of despondency, which is so often visible on the features of those who have lived long, and their fondest hopes have been often crushed. Then came the husband or the father in prime of life, the deep feeling of his manly heart locked up by fortitude and strength of purpose. I could sometimes distinguish the firey zeal of youthful inexperience with sickness and sorrow by the very sound of the door bell. His agonized heart can scarcely brook the delay necessary to gain him admittance. His dear parent, or brother, or sister, or even a beloved bride, or the infant of his early love is touched by the destroyer, disease. His wants, hopes and fears are hurriedly made known. Again the female, though at other times timid and shrinking, has now gathered strength from necessity and is firm in her purpose. Thus this part of my duty became a pleasant study. My heart longed to be of service to them, to one and all, I immediately determined to become a Physician, should an opportunity ever offer. At length I mentioned my wishes to my benefactor. He set before me the care and toil attendant on the profession, the envy and malice often returned where gratitude alone was due, and kindly hinted that I could not read, and consequently could not prepare for the task unless I could receive a liberal education. This served to dampen my newly created hopes, for I had already began to take pride in self-acquired abilities. At length he told me that the Indian Doctors were equally as successful as himself, that I could learn of them, if I ever returned, their manner of using roots and herbs, and probably benefit our race by the knowledge. He jocosely added, this will be a new feature and also a great one in educating yourself. My purpose was instantly taken. The Doctor then informed me that whenever he could find leisure he would himself instruct me somewhat in anatomy, the probable causes of disease in the human frame, its effects upon the body and mind. His instructions were indelibly stamped upon my memory. As soon as opportunity offered, I set myself to work. I laid my plan before the medicine men of more [Page 23] than one tribe and received their instructions, and their blessings. They demonstrated their statements by trials on domestic animals, upon sick friends and often upon ourselves. I soon gained much knowledge that has since been useful to me and also to the poor. When I returned to the settlements of the whites, I gathered and bought up a little lot of medicines; often have I received the heartfelt thanks of the poor of those parts, who had not means to apply to a physician of a higher stamp. I zealously refused all remuneration, except a keepsake was offered. There were but few of my friends who knew that I ever had such a thought. How eagerly I watched each symptom, the progress of the disease, and if arrested by my simple medicine, I carefully noted each change, thereby instructing myself, often acknowledging that practice makes perfect. I could speak several languages, and thereby make myself familiar with the sick emigrant, and many of them have gladly availed themselves of my cheap store, and thus be obliging friends. I should not mention my early practice here, only that I wish to let the public know that I have long had experience in the healing art, with those simple herbs.

How long I remained with this kind gentleman, my memory does not serve me; it may have been a year. I was one day sent to the office of the surgeon, upon an errand, by some of the ladies of the officers of the Post. While passing from the office, a young man who was studying medicine with the Surgeon raised his window and called me. A lad about 16 years of age happened to be near. This lad was asking the young Surgeon if I lived there; when I came up, he, seeing me, said with a sneer of contempt, there comes your colored lover. He was very fond of Mary White, who was a special friend of mine, in consequence of her connexion with the dear Munce family, of whom I have before spoken, and became very jealous of me; consequently he was always tantalizing me with such epithets. When the lad spoke thus, all my Indian nature was aroused, and my very blood boiled in every vein, and my feelings were so intense that I called upon the Great Spirit, and conjured heaven and earth to know where I originated. I picked up a part of a brick, though I scarcely hoped to reach him, yet I aimed at his head with all my might; it reached him just as he happened to turn around to see what I was doing. It cut his lips and knocked out five of his teeth. The doctor had to sew up his lips. His friends made a search to see who was around me, and threatened to prosecute me. The Surgeon quieted my feelings, saying no harm [Page 24] should befall me. They went to my unnatural mother to see what they could do with her. My runaway excursion was not yet settled for, and she said she could not do any thing about it, and they must take my body. She made many complaints about my violent and unconquerable temper, and said she had intended to have me imprisoned, and there whipped and starved, until my spirit should be tamed.

IMPRISONMENT AND CRUEL WHIPPING.

The people were strangers to me, and the fathers of many other boys that I had boxed for the same insult, took advantage of this, and bore testimony against me that I was a dangerous boy when angry. They however spoke of my industrious habits and talents favorably, and upon the whole they concluded to confine me in prison, with now and then a flogging, with little to eat; according to the sentence of Esq. J. Tooley. I heard my sentence with sullen composure. They asked me if I was not sorry; I told them that if their laws and prison had power to keep my body, I was sure I had power over my own tongue; that I could not, and would not talk with them, and when I was sorry it would be before God alone. While I was in prison, a white man came to me, and said he had many things to say to me to which I must listen attentively. He told me that the woman called my mother was a slave, as well as the mother of the two children, but she was set free before the birth of these two children, consequently her two children were free, but I was their slave. This unloosed my tongue, and raised every angry passion of my nature. I loudly asserted that he had brought me from my own home, and had made me a slave; he bade me be quiet until he could tell me all; he then changed his tone, and told me I had a father, probably a white man, but as he did not come to buy me, I was consequently given over as a slave to the children. He said I must never reveal this. I told him I could not and would not make any such promises, for I would be sure to break them, and to spare himself the trouble of trying to console me with such base falsehoods. I told him this woman when angry called me different names; wishing she had never seen the wild savage devils, sometimes even calling me a white woman's child, which, beside her evil treatment, gave me every reason to believe she was not my mother, I told him that some strange mysteries hung over my birth, and I accused him of knowing what it was, [Page 25] and on my knees implored him to unravel it to me if to none other, telling him by so doing he would console me. He turned coldly from me, while I stretched myself on the floor in despair, assuring him my blood was free, and pure. I crawled around where I could look him in the face, telling him he need not fear to rescue me from this place of abuse and digrace, that every step in after life should be to prove it, and honor him, but he said nothing. I then thought he would do nothing for me; I said, well, I will bear it; it will lay me in my grave, and there I shall be free. He was touched with my earnest importunity; gazed upon me a moment, then stooped, and raised me from the floor with his own hand, and he begged me to be calm, to compose the tumult of my feelings, saying it is a pity you should be wronged for the love of money, for let your skin be what it may, you have a noble heart. He promised me he would never wrong me, but strove again to obtain the promise he first wished; but I could not promise; he said he would use his influence to obtain my release; he bid me a kind farewell, wishing me kind friends, and better success for the future. I was then left alone for the night, and a part of the next day, after which I underwent a severe course of punishment, the severest of it being their advice as regarded names or epithets that I might receive, telling me I must even expect it, and bear it too, from the very fact of the woman known as my mother, having been a slave; but as usual I denied her being my mother, told them all I knew of myself before I knew her, which was new to them, and some of my enemies were thus turned to friends; they said it was not unreasonable to suppose that I was an Indian child, taken when small, for the purpose of making me a slave. Some asserted they had heard of such circumstances, and it was easily done, where there was such a diversity of color as there is in the South.

LIBERATED FROM PRISON.

After whipping me until I fainted, they let me go from the prison, and I was allowed to remain with kind friends, who said if they had known of my troubles they would have interposed, and proved me a good child, with the exception of a violent temper which could not be denied; but when treated half right, I was industrious, obedient, gentle and kind; and was free from many faults that beset boys who had not only the advantage of being white, but whose parents moved in the [Page 26] highest circles of society—that my manners were manly in the extreme; that I had many exalted and noble ideas, relative not only to men and things in this world, but also entertained the most elevated and exalted views of God and his attributes; and as I had received no education, other moral, mental, or physical, these thoughts must have been original. This leads me to believe that these ideas must have emanated from the Good Spirit, and that man is immortal, and will live eternally after he leaves this world.

A VISIT TO ALEXANDRIA—THRILLING INTERVIEW WITH THE INDIANS.

One day I walked down to the river, and found Steam Boats from every part of the great valley of the Mississippi. The captain of one of them, bound to Red River, who knew that I was unprotected, and without employment, asked me how I would like a trip to Alexandria, saying he thought it would improve my health and spirits. I told him if I could pay my expenses I would gladly go. I was soon on board, and the boat under weigh. Before we reached the place of destination, I frankly told the Captain my belief respecting my birth, and that I did not wish to return, but rather remain in that country to visit some of the Indian villages—he willingly permitted me to stay, and promised to, say nothing on his return respecting my retreat. I here felt reassured, and though I had no friends present, it was a comfort to know I had no enemies. I soon obtained sundry small jobs, which paid for my board, and something besides. I did not wish to enter into steady employment, as I intended the first opportunity to visit the Indians.

Perhaps I should have stated, that I had seen Indians frequently in Natchez, but soon learned that when any of them came to town I was carefully and closely watched. It appears that some one always gave the necessary information to whoever I lived with, saying I had threatened to run away with them. Permit me to describe my feelings the first time I ever saw Indians. I had just stepped out of a door into the street as they were coming down the street; they were walking slowly, seeming to be looking at the buildings; I appeared nailed to the spot, my heart leaped with joy, yet a choking sensation amounting to pain seized me; confused ideas crowded upon my mind; they were near me, yet I moved not, until the keen eyes of one of them rested upon me; he [Page 27] spoke, the eyes of the whole company turned upon me, and then upon each other, while as it seemed to me they uttered an exclamation of surprise; they came towards me; I was wild with delight, I thought I was their child, that they were seeking for me; I started and held out my hands, tears gushed from my eyes, I addressed them in a language to me unknown before; it was neither English, Spanish, or French; astonished, they spoke kind to me, smoothing my hair with their hands; an explanation now took place, as one could speak English; he said I had asked in Choctaw for my father, saying he had gone and left me, and I was with bad people; that I begged to know if he was not with them. They then asked for my mother. This pained me, I told them she was not my mother; they looked at each other, spoke faster and louder, and looked very angry: there had a crowd of children, and men and women gathered; the Indians loudly asked where and to whom does this child belong? Some one answered to a colored woman. The clouds seemed to grow darker on their wry, yet to me, sweet face, the same one said, to a slave woman, and he is a slave. The Indian held his hands high above his head and said, "but white man lie, he no good, him no slave no, bad white man steal him, his skin is red;" this was repeated in imperfect English by them all—me I love him—the crowd were some smoking, laughing, some mocking, angry and cursing. The Indians conversed in a low tone together, here some of the crowd interfered, and separated me from my new, but dear friends—while, all the time, "bad white man lie, he steal him, he no nigger, him Indian boy," now and then reached my ears. I was then torn from them. My feelings towards them I cannot attempt to explain.

I here learned that the Indians often visited the village, that they came here and fished, and sold their fish to the inhabitants, and I determined to make their acquaintance here, and so get an invitation to their camps. As I still retained a love for the hook and line, it was just in my hand. The first Indian I met, assisted me in a friendly manner, which I returned, and was soon happy among them, for they seemed to regard me as a companion; they did not even ask for or look for other blood in me. I tasked my memory in bringing to mind, words often on my tongue though I had no recollection of their meaning. They told me it was the Choctaw tongue. I was over anxious to gain the friendship of those who spoke a little English, and as soon as I was sure of their confidence, I gave to them a history of my sorrows in part; it was night, and we were gathered around the camp fire, one of them serving as interpreter. [Page 28] I had scarcely began before the pipe was laid by, one saying their hearts were sorry, and they could not smoke; the elder ones bent their eyes on the ground, their features settled into an immovable silence, their arms were folded upon their breasts; their very silence said to me, this is but another lesson in the deceitfulness of the pale face. The eyes of the younger ones were fixed upon me, and their features manifested a restlessness, and they manifested signs of revenge; they grasped their tomahawks firmly; my emotion soon prevented my proceeding. I showed them my back: that expression, eagh! eagh! eagh! so significant of high resolves, contempt, and indignation, &c., escaped the lips of the older, while an angry wail went forth from the young. Their leader spoke when all was silent; their interpreter gave me what follows: "Pale face alway say he friend, poor Indian get money, bad pale face get fire-water, then he friend; Indian got no money, then he got no friend; but he got hunting-ground, pale face want it, he fight a little, give little this, and little that, last poor Indian take fire water, he then loses sense, then white man get his home. The Great Spirit gave pale face children, houses, cattle, but this no enough; he love black slave. Indian skin no white, but dark red, so he think Indian make good slave; so he try him; but he no make slave; so bad white man steal papoose, may be he make good slave. "No, no, no, bad white man, he no good, he speak with a forked tongue." While he was speaking, not a motion was made, or any other sound heard; nor a leaf trembled; as he ceased my ears were almost deafened with the loud yells of indignation that burst upon me as they sprang to their feet and began dancing around me. This was a scene novel to me; I had roused their feelings for me, but knew not how to quell them.

It was late before we laid down in our wigwams; we arose very early; they said they could not sleep, and were sorry for their brother's son, and their fears plainly showed that they were ill at ease. We washed ourselves all over, thoroughly; they gathered around the fire, standing in a circle, holding their left hand up to the Great Spirit; said a few words in their own tongue deeply serious, wet the fore finger with the same hand, dipped it in the ashes, beginning at the corner of the eye drew it downwards, imitating the trickling of a tear; their leader then spoke a few words, the others imitating him, at holding up the same hand, their eyes fixed on the morning sky as their words fell from their lips. They looked upon me as though they were reading my heart, instead of searching my features. I did not know how to act, but the interpreter [Page 29] told me they were invoking the Great Spirit for me, and expressing sorrow for my situation. They then very gravely informed me that I must not fish for them any more, as I had caught more fish than they, and they were convinced that the Great Spirit had given me this as a gift to supply my wants, and he would be angry with them if they accepted of any which I could sell. To this I undertook to object telling them I had some little money and was their visitor, and had partaken of their bread, but still they answered, we also have partaken of your fish. My interpreter here motioned me to be silent; they believed a supernatural power would uphold me, and that these difficulties were suffered to gather around the path to test my honor; that the God of good, (meaning good and bad persons, habits, &c., &c.) of the pale face, and the bad alike, had come before me; if I choose the good; the Great Spirit would deliver me; I then wished to be cheerful, but as long as they let the ashes stay upon their faces, I scarcely spoke; but when this was taken off, I felt at liberty, and attempted to amuse them by telling anecdotes about myself which pleased them so much that they had a great powwow about it, and they were in perfect ecstacies about them.

ANECDOTES RELATED BY ME AT THAT TIME.

I had stolen away one morning and repaired to the spot where I had hidden my fish poles under a flat-bottomed boat. On touching the poles I heard the cry which was like what I had always supposed to proceed from a negro baby, and which gave me the most horrid sensations, though I had never seen one, but had often heard white people speak of the peculiarity of their cry. Not doubting, I stooped down to examine more closely; it seemed in a sitting posture, leaning forward, looked young, and I felt all my former disgust return. I touched it with a pole; again it uttered a hideous cry; I snatched up my poles and returned to the lake. I could not but reflect that if it was human it was sensible of pain, cold and hunger. I was touched with pity, and returned, determining to serve it; but I could not reach it, it seemed frightened at me; I relinquished the idea and went back to the lake; I passed several hours in watching, expecting to see it emerge from its concealment, on being left alone. About one o'clock, a Spaniard came to me; I told him my exploit, spoke of its cries, and endeavoured to interest [Page 30] him in its favour; he stooped down and examined closely, and said "ah, this Johny Crapo," and to my amazement drew forth a large bull-frog, whose head was nearly as large as my head; it still kept on crying like a negro baby. The Spanish man killed and dressed it, and sold it to some Frenchman for three dollars: another one opposite kept hallooing, "chubbe, chubbe, chubbe," I am coming; I started to go to it, and on the way passed two large mocasin snakes, but they did not molest me; I killed the frog and sold it for half a dollar. While I was fishing, I made a little basket to put my fish in, and when I went to put my fish in it, a large

mocasin* jumped at me, but I soon dispatched him; I was afterwards at-
tacked by two of their snakeships who had stretched themselves on a log
that had fallen across a small river; they were after my fish; I killed one
and the other escaped from me—this restored cheerfulness, and the leader
drew a moral from this, saying, my enemies took me for a negro baby, but
it will all come out like the frog story. The Spanish man told the joke, and
my enemies often tormented me with it. I then would sit by the side of the
lake and watch the frogs. I then imitated them in a coarse bass voice; the
head one answered "knee deep," and another one called out, "fried bacon,"
"more rum," another, "snatch him," the head frog called out "toleration," his
mate halloed, "flam him." They were so delighted that they entered heartily
into the feast and dance.

I then returned to the village where I made many friends, French, Spanish, and one English family especially, who made me acquainted with a
gentleman who was very wealthy, who resided in Mississippi; claimed me
as his cousin, he was related to the family who became so friendly to me.
Mrs. Kitchen, was a sister of this gentleman, which would have made us
relatives. Captain Brown was going up to Natchitoches in a keel boat; he
engaged me to accompany him. After having proceeded some miles up the
river, I went on deck, surveying the scenery as we passed, having a pair of
high heel shoes on made me very clumsy, and I fell overboard; the cur-
rent was swift here and carried me down; as I was not an expert swimmer,
I strangled; a young man saw me sinking, and dived in and rescued me
from drowning; I came up out of the water farther down the river than he
had expected; he by using all his exertions saved me as I was sinking the
third time; I had not until this moment had any acquaintance with either
the young man, or his father, but a brotherly feeling sprang up between
us; we made our trip and returned [Page 31] together, his father living opposite Alexandria, I went home with him; the young man proposed that
I should assist him at the ferry; I worked with them three months; my Indian friends often visited me, and informed me that many of the Choctaws
lived in Mississippi, and advised me to visit them.

---

* A species of poisonous snakes.

RETURN TO NATCHEZ,

About this time a gentleman living in Natchez landed here; he recognized me, and coaxed me to return with him, saying I had many friends in Natchez who were anxious about me, and had been much concerned about my absence. I found that to visit the Indian country I must return by the way of Natchez. He promised that my unnatural mother should have no controul over me; he said I should go to a trade and be used well. When I left Alexandria, many friends followed me to the boat, sending their best wishes. I returned to Natchez, having been absent nine months; my friends greeted me with smiles, complimenting me with my improvement.

MY SUFFERINGS IN CONNECTION WITH LEARNING THE BLACKSMITH'S TRADE.

By the advice of many individuals, I commenced the blacksmith trade with McCaffrey and Jeter; but at length when they dissolved, Mr. Jeter advised me to go and complete my trade with his brother-in-law, Mr. Russell. I had entertained such entire confidence in him that my spirits sank within me. I was totally unprepared for his unkind treatment. I wept again and again over his cruel conduct to me, and found that suspicion and jealousy, so contrary to my nature, and which had hitherto been strangers to me, had taken possession of my heart. I was entirely unconscious of other persons suffering the same painful emotions, which were gnawing like canker worms upon my heart, crushing down my young hopes; I was becoming poorer in flesh every day, but I still continued steadily at my work, to drive away my bad feelings. I do not know how old I was, but they made me three steps to raise me high enough to blow the bellows, and strike upon the anvil. Some months had passed in this fearful manner, when at length one day Mr. Russell came to me, and ordered me to strip for the whip; in vain I begged to [Page 32] know what I had done to merit such usage; he only answered me with angry oaths, so loud that I stood in dread in silence, and obeyed, determining in my mind that this should be the last time I would do it. He used a whip known in the South as an overseer's whip. I fell to the floor after a few of the first blows, they were so severe; they seemed to take away my breath, and I thought my life; but I retained my consciousness of it until he ceased; I tried but could not arise, but my cries for help at first were so heart-rending, that although the shop was closed; people hearing my cries rushed through the back way and forced him to stop; they raised me up, but I knew it not; I had fainted; they took me away, and washed my body, bathed my wounds, which brought back a sense of pain, but it was only to faint again, while the blood flowed fast. On coming to myself again, I vomited freely, but soon fainted again from pain and loss of blood. A physician was called; he seemed alarmed at my situation, and said it might cause my death, the vomiting and fainting for twenty-four hours in spite of all their efforts continuing. Russell seemed very much alarmed, but I could not bear the sight of him, and would not permit him to come near me; he then gave orders to have every thing possible done for my recovery. What alarmed him most was that the people told him that if I died in consequence of his cruel treatment, they would put the law in force against him, which would be without any formal trial to tar and feather him, ride him on a rail, and then hang him without judge or jury, or the benefit of clergy.

My freinds watched over me with all the tenderness that they would if I had been their own child. For the first three weeks I was compelled to lie on my stomach, and when I could change my position, I was compelled to rest on my knees, so that I have at least been in a humble position once in my life, if no more, from the force of circumstances; but I feel grateful to the Good Spirit that he has given me a heart to bow before him, and adore his goodness, and I shall even be thankful that he raised me up such kind friends; for had he not, I must have died, and now been sleeping beneath the green sod of the valley. The wounds in my back and sides were so deep that you could in some places see through into my stomach. My back was a complete running sore; it was well known that I was perfectly well on the morning that this circumstance took place, and then to see me in this situation, it was talked over again and again; and the people became so exasperated that they told Russell that if he did not leave, they would ride him out of town on a rail; this so alarmed him that he picked up his duds and moved away immediately, [Page 33] He died a miserable death, being drowned in a ditch, in a fit of intoxication; making my prophecies true that God would punish him for his savage treatment of me. "Though hand join in hand the wicked shall not go unpunished." My friends took me away from Russell home with them, where I remained until I recovered.

I had offers on every hand for employment; Mr. McCaffrey, who had ever been my friend, proposed that I should finish the blacksmithing with him; here I was treated as a member of his family; I worked very hard for some months, when I had a violent attack of the bilious fever, the only sickness I ever had in my life; I was almost unconscious, and suffered much for three weeks. I recovered slowly, and lingered some time under the effects, and the physicians advised me to travel for my recovery. I had some money, and insisted on the Doctor's taking some; and left for a while, starting for Brandywine; but my money giving out, threw me again upon my own resources. One night, being tired, I stopped at a little cottage where they treated me very kindly, and gave me a poor old horse which they had turned out upon the commons. I rode him on the level road, and walked up and down the hills; by this means I was enabled to reach Brandywine springs, where I soon made friends, and spent the fall and winter. I had sometimes visited ball rooms and acted as a prompter, my voice being strong and distinct. I was employed as a prompter. In the spring I returned to my employer, Mr. McCaffrey, and finished my trade.

Many hours I occupied my mind in beating the time of some favorite tune with my sledge hammer. I seemed to work faster, and then it soothed the care of my mind, serving to drive away angry and sorrowful thoughts. Soon after I returned, I was chosen to play for the Natchez Cadets, and they elected me Fife Major—gave me my uniform, and on the fourth of July, 1830 or '31, (if I mistake not,) my feelings were of mingled gratitude and pride, for as we marched through the street I saw mortified countenances on every hand. I received many congratulations from friends and the highest hopes of the future took possession of my mind. I became a great favorite, loved on one hand as strongly as I was hated and oppressed on the other. My boss soon noticed the manner I executed music with my hammer; it was commented upon by the workmen, and by customers, and I got a dime a tune, many times even fifty cents, keeping at my work, throwing in now and then some imitations. Many horse shoes I made in this manner, and from my presents I managed to keep an extra suit of fashionable clothes, preferring white [Page 34] linen for summer, as it suited the redness of my skin. And when the shop was not crowded, I had the privilege of stopping at five or six o'clock, and taking a pleasant stroll with my friends, who seemed to vie with each other to cause me by their kindness to forget the obscurity of my birth; but it seemed to haunt most of my waking hours; otherwise I should have been as happy as need be. I still continued practicing music, adding the clarionet to my practice.

Late in the fall, some of the Indians I had seen at Brandywine came to see me. Mr. McCaffrey received them kindly, and told me I was free for the day. I had the inexpressible pleasure of a walk with them through the principal streets, introducing them to my friends, and as they were well behaved, we were invited to visit some of the grandees, where they publicly acknowledged me. This was very gratifying, as enemies always looked black to see me walking or talking with respectable white people, but now they had no time to look this way, seeming not to see me. We returned to Mr. McCaffrey's, had something to eat and retired. On rising I was warmly greeted by my shop mates, who told me my last march was the best one I ever made; but behind my back some white men who wished to see me held as a slave, sought out the Indians, and said, "whites no like black man, he like Indian best: eugh, was the Indian's reply." All silent, the Indian said with a little hesitation, "white man why you tell me this." The white man answered, "we see you Indians and slave boy walking together, eugh!" Again the white man proceeded, "may be you no know he slave. We tell you we like Indian heap" "eugh! No, said the Indian, we no know he slave—may be you no know it—may be white man lie heap." They knew they alluded to me, and angrily told them they would not believe, and soon left the city. Time moved on in this pleasant manner, without much interruption. I was steady at work—was well treated, nothing of importance occuring that I need relate, until the next fall, except that I began to save my money and to extra jobs. Such mending as I could do, my boss gave me the money for it, and also for making pot hooks, andirons, &c. when one day my heart was gladdened as the sound of boba-helah (which is friend, in Choctaw,) fell on my ear. There was a large party camped on the bluff, and had sent these after me. I was permitted to go after doing a job. I was very anxious to go, and when my work was done, I not only had the satisfaction of going with the consent of all hands, but had their congratulations on being the cause of the approaching festivity, as they were making [Page 35] great preparations. They came for me at the house; I returned with them to the camp, from whence the whole company proceeded through the principal streets; I walked in front with the principal Chief, the oldest men followed next, the braves bringing up the rear. We walked quietly through the street, back to the camp on the bluffs; there I spent three days before they would let me go; they then conducted me home; I waited at the door until men, women, and children bid me adieu. I thought they did this to gratify themselves and please me, but I found it had great bearing in the minds of many, knowing that one Indian can tell another, and they told all that met them that this brother's son may be big Chief's son. They told me to learn my trade, and then come and see my people, and learn them. My extra jobs began to increase so as to employ every moment. I had learned to make gridirons, tributes, or iron stands, &c., and picked up all the scraps of iron, saved all the old horse shoes about the shop, which I began welding together, working late and early, for business in my line was increasing. I soon finished welding, and had iron enough to make a pair of shovel and tongs. My boss bought it for nails, giving me in return as much new iron, and enough over to make a pair of andirons. When I got them finished, I received $3 a piece for the three articles. My health was good—strength increasing every day. In this manner five years passed away, which released me from my trade. Mr. McCaffrey gave me a good suit of clothes, and by my own industry, and through his indulgence, I had saved {$}300. My friends had often told me to get papers or indentures to shew I had served my trade and was released honorably. My boss was very willing; but some opposed it. I looked back on the last five years, and felt I had enjoyed a sweet calm—my sky had long been clear—a cloud seemed gathering in the distance, from which a fearful storm arose.

MY FIRST EFFORT AT KEEPING HOUSE.

A friend offered me a house on reasonable terms, which I fitted up with little expense, for my friends made me many presents in the household line. The front room had been a barber shop. I hired a barber, (William Hayden by name) to carry it on, whose custom was quite extensive. Here I kept young bachelor's hall, being determined that the lessons I had taken in my adversity, should now be of some use to me. I served as market boy and chambermaid.

[Page 36]I had marched a few times with the Natchez Fencibles while at my trade, and now appeared with the Natchez Guards; soon after, Adam's Light Guards. This drew my acquaintances to my house. My prosperity seemed to gall my enemies sorely, so much so, that I was often abused and insulted in the street by black and white, when even at the head of companies. This was very painful to me, and served to mar the peace I had so long enjoyed without much interruption. Some time had elapsed since I left Mr. McCaffrey, and I had not got my indentures yet—I was much opposed. My enemies said that I could make money fast, and could afford to buy myself of the woman, and thus settle the dispute. This mortified me very much; indeed my feelings I do not attempt to describe. I was waited upon for an answer to the degrading proposition. What! I, with the consciousness of possessing a good heart, a fine mind; nature having lavished on me talents of the highest order, uncultivated as they were, they were beginning to be highly approved by many. Could I stoop to this? I was exceedingly careful in my manners, and now that the boy was somewhat polished in the man, why should they persecute me still? I firmly refused them; not that I valued the money so much; no, to have had them cease tormenting me, I would not have begrudged twice the amount; but to have it said that I had to buy my flesh and blood and this lofty spirit!—Oh! horrible thought! it stung my inmost soul, and almost maddened me into despair.

ENTICEMENT OF THE COLOURED WOMAN.

The colored womam, of whom I have had reason to speak so often, had of late appeared to be uncommonly friendly. I felt that something was wrong. Having mentioned it to some of my friends, they argued that she had become repentant and wished to ask my forgiveness; others thought that she might probably confess and bring to light my true percentage, if I would only give her a chance; they advised me to do all I could to bring about at least a seeming reconciliation. I promised to do nothing to hinder it, but could not feel willing to even try to bring it about. Neither did I. Soon after, she dropped into my house, looked at my things, and made many comments, being in a fine humor; she invited me to come to her house; but before I had made a definite answer, she asked if I thought I had ever seen Sally Kelly before I saw her. I immediately recollected what Sally had said to me when I was between [Page 37] ten and twelve years old, though I had no recollection of seeing her when so young, yet I led her to believe that I had. When somewhere about the age named, I met a very black woman in the street; she seemed very glad to see me, and yet big tears stood in her eyes; she asked me to shake hands with her because she was my first black mamma. One black mamma was too many, and I wished to be off, yet her words fast chained me there; she looked about the street, and up to the windows, I thought to see if any person was looking at her, still holding on to my hand, said to herself, (but my ears were open) "yes, this son of the broad forest Chief was brought to me first; though I was then and am yet very wicked, yet I never wronged an innocent child, and his bitter lamentations for his parents, especially his father, still ring in my ears." I had become impatient to know all she knew of me. She ceased speaking, but gazing inquiringly into my eyes, said, "you are young, and if you should tell they would beat me to death." She said if I would not tell until I was grown, she would then tell me all she knew of me; she bade me follow her down the alley and she would talk to me. She then said "Yes, child, the white man's blood possesses no more freedom than yours, yet they have made no distinction between you and the negro slave." She then said the white man who found me, and her master were great friends; that he had been on one occasion some time from home, and on returning he brought me there and wished to see her master alone; (she was the only woman there) so when they were alone, she slipped up and listened, for my appearance had excited her curiosity, for she had often heard them speak of stealing Indian children and making slaves of them, and she heard him say to her master, "Yes, I can get the shiners for him, for the old Chief is away and will search for him when he returns, and I can easily say I found him, and he will pay me for my trouble, and a present besides, and then I shall not have to raise him or run the risk of his dying." And as his colored woman and himself had parted in a quarrel, it was decided that I should be told that he had bought you below, and that I must learn you to talk, as it seemed you did not know how to speak with any sense; my master then asked him if you was old * Bill Chubbee's son; he answered yes, and they, laughing, swore he had made a lucky hit. I then left the key-hole and sought the child, who was afraid of me and would not speak. They soon told me some tale about you, little dreaming that I knew you had been kidnapped by them. I was not to take [Page 38] you out myself; you seemed to be very anxious to go out, and ate very little, and either screamed and cried, or sat in sullen silence. I often listened to find out any thing concerning you, and at length found that your father supposed you had been destroyed by wild beasts, or stolen by some warlike tribe: he had vowed vengeance on whoever had the child. Now came many consultations; he feared to take you home lest he should suffer. Your father had not thought of your being with the white man: he believed they were friends. They now began to talk of keeping you as a slave: my own conscience smote me, and I threw out my hints, thinking to frighten them; but they carelessly told me I knew too much, saying they must find the child a mother, but I was so black that I would not do. I was glad of it. The man had long promised to set his woman free; he now offered her freedom if she would say she gave birth to this child, when they moved to Natchez. To this she agreed, and he set her free. We all moved

---

* A name the whites had given Mosholeh Tubbee on account of large size.

to Natchez; she became known as the mother of you." She then turned to me and said, "Now if you can keep this until you are a man, I will tell you more; yes, you will know it all and be free and respected. I always knew it, and that has kept my tongue still; but I could not help telling you I was your mother first, and when you are about they are afraid I will tell it all, for I always took your part. So good bye; my heart is easier now; come and see me, and remember what I promise when you are grown, so mind your tongue."

When alone, I endeavoured to stamp her words in my brain, saying them over to myself, for fear I should forget them. I had not seen Sally for some years; as some stolen goods were found to be harboured by her, she had to leave the city unexpectedly and unknown to me, and I had heard nothing of her since. I had never named her communication with me, and now that I was thus questioned, I determined to make use of my knowledge. I accordingly accepted an invitation to come to her house, and eat and talked with her. When I told her Sally was my mother before she was, she was silent some moments, and then said, "Yes, but we did not think you remembered her, or being with her at least." But she refused to tell me where Sally was, but she told me a story corroborating Sally's, alleging she had to do as her master wished. She opened a bureau-drawer and showed me a suit of fine clothes that the man had left when he went away, saying he expected to return when he left, but she should keep the clothes for his son; she told me her children were his. She then said that [Page 39] to the negro, but that any other child the whites could steal, that was not white, was just as much a slave as the negro; she then said she was going to tell me a little more and trust to my own good heart to do her justice. I motioned her to proceed, and she said that a white man had got me from old Bill Chubbee, the chief of some tribe of Mississippi Indians, and that because he was so big and fat they called him Chubbee; that he failed to come for me. Every thing turned against the man: he had prepared to give her children a part of his fortune. (At this time eatables were brought in, and I drank coffee freely, while she after waiting as long as she could, adds) "So he just gave you to them, and now we will do what is right; you are a fine young man, about 25 or 26, I think, though some may say not over 23." While she was speaking, a painful stupor seemed to come over me; I arose to go, but she detained me almost forcibly, saying I must hear her out; I sat down for I could scarcely stand, and I tried to rally myself, for I feared my feelings had overcome me; my head seemed ready to burst, while a dizzy sleepiness look possession of me; the old woman finished by saying, "You can make the children a few presents, and do something for me and we will give you up, and thus stop this quarrel." I told her I would never give a farthing as a present, or pay for the freedom with which I was born. I again rose but could not walk or scarcely stand. She told me I must not go, that I was too sleepy. I must go to bed; scarcely knowing what I did, I pulled off my coat and vest, and threw myself on the bed and went to sleep.

When I awoke it was to a sense of the keenest pain; I seemed smarting. Could it be I felt the lash; yes, writhing under its torture, as it was laid upon my flesh, I endeavoured to rise, but I could not move. The blows seemed to fall heavy and fast, but how could this be possible? I had been too happy, I must be suffering under some dreadful disease, I thought I had the night-mare. But then by this time I had gathered my scattered senses and remembered that I was in bed, and found I was on my face, the sheet wound close about my head, my hands and feet tied fast to the bedstead. I remembered where I was, and our conversation, I then knew it was no night-mare, no dream, and I struggled with all my might to unwrap my head; at length I partly succeeded, and saw light again; the blows ceased, and oh, horror! there she stood, she whose guest I was, and now her prisoner. Even to this day, which I think of, or relate this disgusting scene, the same feelings return; I felt sick at heart; She soon spoke like this: "Sir I [Page 40] ken this plan to show you, you have a master; you have refused to give me anything for yourself, just as I expected, though I thought I would try you; you are so ungovernable that no one will buy you, and the people are fools enough to think that you do not belong to us, but I have got you now in my own power in spite of your fraud or cunning, and no craftiness of yours can release you. No, indeed; nothing but your word that you will buy yourself will do; I will take your word for what a slave man is worth; and now promise me quickly, and be like an Indian in keeping your word. You would hate to own you was whipped by me after you came out a fine gentleman. and if you please I will say nothing about it; if not, I will beat you until you are glad to promise." I then said "are you prepared, beastly woman, to answer to God and man for my life? I now solemnly say, I will never promise that." She then "saying you are in my power," began to lay on the blows. Now that I discovered my foe had tied me and my senses had returned, the reality of my disgraceful situation was plain before me, together with the smart of the keen lash seemed to give me lion-like strength, and with a few desperate leaps I succeeded in tearing the bedstead in pieces, breaking the cord that bound my feet, tearing up a pair of cloth pants for which I had just paid seventeen dollars. With the part to which my hands were fastened I felled the old woman, leaving her to pick up herself, while I rushed to the door where I soon gnawed my right hand loose, and seeing a friend of her's coming to her from a distance, I picked up a piece of brick and levelled him. My jaws and teeth were tired, and by way of experiment I found I could saw a rope in two with two bricks. I was soon loose but almost naked and bloody; with little hesitation I walked to her door; it was locked, I picked up a stick of wood, knocked in her window, and went in, got my coat and vest; but then I had no pants. I opened the drawer and took the suit she had shown me, dared her to move while I washed and dressed in these clothes, and left the house forever.

The Officers of the United States Army kindly protected me from any insulting correction which my enemies might have undertaken to inflict upon me. I returned peacably to my own house, and attended to my own affairs as usual. My friends all said that I had suffered too much from her already, and that I had served her just right. But my enemies undertook to force me to buy myself; saying let me be what I might, I was given to the colored woman, and she had a right to me; and that it was impossible to sell me, for I was so well known and had [Page 41] so many friends who all respected me too much to buy me, and all others were afraid of me.

A SHORT VISIT TO NEW ORLEANS.

I left Natchez, determined, though I had good friends there, to seek others abroad. I proceeded to New Orleans. I soon made acquaintance with Mr. C. F. Hosea, Captain of the Old Louisiana Volunteers, who proved a very true and faithful friend. He introduced me to his musicians, who were very good friends; especially his drum-major, Mr. J. Noble. I played with them on the eighth of January, at a sham fight, where I found myself very much at home.

I remained here but a very short time however, and went up the river to Vicksburg, where there was a party given, and they hired me to play on the flute, for which they gave me one hundred dollars for the night. I had several good jobs here, as well as good friends; yet some of the lower class began to find fault with my visiting, as news began to circulate concerning my fate at Natchez. My friends, however, did all they could for me. I staid near three months, saving while there three hundred dollars.

It seemed that by an act of their state laws, all free people not white, must pay a license for living in the state. I was about to return to Natchez to make a visit among my friends. Some, however, wished that I would never go back again, but my mind led me back. My friends heartily greeted and welcomed me, but my enemies soon beset me again, and the officers of the city determined that I should take out a license in less than twenty-four hours, or leave the state. Several gentlemen of high standing in the city, viz. Esquire Tooley, General John A. Quitman, Mr. Ferrady, and Dr. Carr, united in their advice that I had better go and see Edward Turner, Judge of Probate. He gave me much good advice. He thought I had better on the whole, leave the state, as I should be constantly subject to annoyances from my enemies. I was grieved in heart, and determined, license or no license, I would leave the State; for although it was the supposed land of my birth, some of its sons were my bitter enemies. I had had the command of the military music; several colored men had applied for a place in the band, and on being refused would vent their spite on me, with their fists and canes. I paid several bills to the physicians, from these assaults, but at length told them I had the receipt in the pain and bruises, and they [Page 42] must get their money from those to whom these liberties were allowed, or from their masters, who when they had the bills to pay, would put a stop to their outrages.

I visited Mrs. Munce again, and her kind son-in-law, Mr. Cyrus Marsh, who had always been very kind to me. While visiting my acquaintances, some of the gentlemen proposed that a petition should be drawn up, and let all sign it who wished me to stay, and have it presented to the Court. They stated that I was not only worthy of citizenship but was of an unexceptionable character; that it was greatly desired by the ladies and gentlemen that I should remain, and enjoy the liberty of a citizen; also all the Military Companies were very anxious for my stay, as I was of great use to them; my enemies said if I could get so many signers they would give it up and say no more about it. I was willing to make the trial, and sure of success, gladly improved the opportunity of letting my enemies hear the high sounding titles of my friends. The aged matrons stepped forth to aid me; the mothers, the young and blooming wives; yes, many beautiful maidens, blushingly added their names to my list; all greeted me with wishes for success, and many tears were shed in supplication for me. My list was soon more than filled by dozens. I took it to the Clerk's office. Mr. A. North, and received a certificate for which I gave {$}3 with direction to go to Jackson, in order to get the Governor to sign it. I here met my friend Mr. Bob Shelby, and several other friends, who received me very kindly. They were astonished to see me there, and inquired "what brought you here"? "A fool's errand," said I, "and as I know you to be my friends, I ask your advice." I then stated that I had been prevailed upon, by several of the citizens of Natchez, and the officers of the Court of Adams County, to accept a certificate of good character from them, and get it signed by the Governor, and then present it to the legislature, petitioning them to grant me the privilege of living in the state, without being brought under the laws enacted for the African people. I stated that I had so far complied with their request, but had concluded to drop it and seek a home abroad. All answered, "that is right; exactly right." "What!" said Mr. Shelby, "will they ask you to stoop so low? they thus seek to cause you to assist in your own disgrace! Yes, leave the state! what has she ever done for you? I have thought I could play on the flute, but if I could play an instrument as I have heard you play, the world should be my home. Take courage and a bright future awaits you. They are pleased with you in Louisiana; return to them [Page 43] again; seek your fortune among them." They made up a contribution and gave me, wishing me a long and happy life. I complied with their advice, and immediately returned to Natchez, to take my leave of my old friends. While remaining here a little time to close up my business, an awful Tornado occurred.

AN AWFUL TORNADO.

I could but exclaim, Oh! my native city, I have seen you blessed with riches and prosperity, and in my adversity you turned on me your back, and I have lived to see you prostrated, laid low by the hand of him who tempers the wind to the shorn lamb. Oh! that your sons had dealt in righteousness; that you might have escaped this outpouring of the weather, or at least have been better prepared to meet your doom. My language cannot describe the feelings of my heart, as I gazed from the hill down on the ruins. I was, at the time the wind came, in the house of A. P. Merrill, in company with a relative of Mrs. Merrill, John Francis Jurault by name. As dinner was nearly ready, we sauntered out on the back gallery. I had made Mr. Merrill's little son some popguns which he brought out. The balls were hanging on the China trees, and Jurault bantered me to shoot at them with him. This was about half an hour before the storm. I noticed a peculiarity, in the lightning that I had never observed before, and as I listened to the steady rolling of the deep-toned thunder, a strange awe crept over me. I said to John Francis, "listen! the very thunder can speak! and it is now admonishing us that we are spending our time foolishly when we should be thinking about God." "Poh! nonsense, said he, we are only trying to make noise enough to drown its bellowing." It had begun in the South, but was fast spreading to the North. As it neared the West it commenced blowing hard, growing very dark. Mr. Merrill now came home! haste had nearly exhausted his strength; he stopped a moment on the gallery; the wind seemed to take away his breath; I raised him up, caught him and rushed into the house; the table was set, and candles were lighted because of the darkness. The ladies had fled up stairs. And now the wind came from the North, the low, angry voice of the thunder sending dread into our very hearts; the house trembled so violently that I chose the open air, placing myself under the large tree, clasping it with my arms to keep my position. The heavens grew darker still, and daylight seemed shut out. I heard as it were a loud [Page 44] explosion over head; again louder, and the third one seemed not only to deafen us, but laid prostrate much of the city. The tall tree seemed kissing the earth in humble resignation to the will of its Maker. In a few moments the dreadful rage somewhat abated, and I with difficulty reached the house, the door of which they had been unable to shut. All was upside down; indeed the lights were extinguished, the dinner table was upset, leaving the dinner on the floor, and throwing the doors wide open, (even the folding doors in the parlour, in spite of the lock) the furniture was all out of place, and a great part of it lay in heaps in and about the stairway; even the dining table was there, the table cloth hanging in one of the hinges. The ladies could not get down, the windows were gone, and the beautiful curtains, which had cost {$}100 a piece, were also gone; although they were hung with golden rings, yet the tempests had torn them away; the furniture was cleared from the stairway; the ladies in sorrow and weeping descended to the scene of desolation, which but a few hours ago was filled with tranquil pleasure; yet we were filled with thankfulness that our lives were spared through this awful hour.

SECOND VISIT TO NEW ORLEANS.

Soon after this terrible catastrophe, I took all and went down to New Orleans, where I made my home about four years.

I soon attached myself to Charles F. Hosea's Company or the Louisiana Guards, which afterwards changed their name to Washington Guards. I discharged my duties honorably, and gained the confidence and esteem of many warm hearted persons. I was elected Fife Major for the Washington Battallion, and as evidence of it I insert a true copy of the order.

SPECIAL ORDER.

Head Quarters Regt. Louisiana Volunteers,

New Orleans. 1st May, 1844.

W. McCAREY* is hereby appointed Fife Major of the Field Music of [Page 45] the Regt. Louisiana Volunteers with full power to regulate said field music agreeably to law and the usual custom in such matters.

By order of
COL. JAMES H. DAKIN.

---

* William McCarey was the name by which I was called by the woman in whose hands I had been placed, and by which I was generally known at the South.

BLACKSMITHING IN NEW ORLEANS.

I here met my friend, Mr. Crane, with whom I had been acquainted in Natchez, and made arrangements to work with him at blacksmithing, as he had charge of Leed's Foundry. I continued steady at my business, making many improvments, until I had not only perfected the common blacksmithing but had acquired a good knowledge of the machinist business. Thus I continued to work for three years.

ROOMS FITTED UP—PARTNERSHIP FORMED—BAND TRAINED, &c. &c.

I rented rooms of a gentleman by the name of Pease in 2nd Municipality, on Circus Street, which proved a very pleasant location. I fitted up my rooms quite handsomely, and if they lacked anything in style or richness, it was my particular care to see that they did not in cleanliness. The smallest article was ever in its own place; everything being in perfect order. My acquaintance was not at this time as extensive as it was destined to become; but I strove to keep the friendship I had already gained, by strictly attending to all business or matters, which in any wise concerned me. Our pay-day was the first of the month, and the parade days were every Sunday; this was the custom of the city,—and custom I find grants license to please herself, whether right or wrong. Many times (having been ordered out at 6 o'clock and commenced parade at 8) I have led the company through the parade back to the drillroom, took my leave of them,—set out for my own room; and if I succeeded in getting there, I considered myself very fortunate indeed; for I generally served two or three companies a day, in pleasure excursions, &c. My Southern friends will remember the little Picayune complimented me often, for being pleasantly aroused from their sweet dreams, as they were luxuriating in a Sunday morning nap, after a week's toil and anxiety in which they could scarcely find time to indulge in sleep necessary to strengthen and invigorate the weary mind. Many [Page 46] good words have not only the Picayune, but other papers given me;—for which I was, and am still and ever will be a thousand times obliged. They prophesied pleasure, fame, and wealth, if I would pursue a steady, straight-forward course. This I truly endeavored to do. As I had much leisure time through the day in some parts of the week, I determined to take care of some of these leisure moments and turn them to my advantage. I had an eye upon a friend of mine, and Italian by birth, who was dealing in fruit; I saw he was faithful to his business, attentive to his customers, and withal an excellent manager, yet had never made much stir in the world. He was very fond of me indeed, and had proved himself my friend. His name was Lazarus (a very good name indeed, but no better than he who bore it.) I accordingly would drop into his store when unemployed, and if I found him busy would lay to and help him. So five or six weeks passed. At length it was proposed that we should go in as partners; and it was no quicker said than done. Lazarus and myself were partners to our full satisfaction; but I still attended to my professional duties.

Mr. Noble was my drummer, in whom I had the greatest confidence. I had a band who could not be excelled, and whom I could leave, if occasion required, though I endeavored to be at my post as much as possible; at least always if in the city.

I thought I should like to see Havana, or at least the trees which bore the delicious fruit we were selling. I accordingly took passage on a fruit schooner. Being some little acquainted with the captain and crew, I had a pleasant voyage; and soon had the liberty of strolling through that garden of dainties, feasting my eyes and appetite thereon. In the meantime I obtained my fruit, and prepared to return. I here formed many acquaintances whom I still remember with pleasure.

We enlarged our trade considerably, and our customers increased, and they often acknowledged that a few good tunes interspersed among the choicest of fruit, was just the thing. Here and at my rooms I made many new acquaintances, and though I have forgotten many of their names, yet their images and kindness continue to live in my heart; though some of them rest with the dead. Peace to their memory.

FREQUENT EXCURSIONS TO THE NEIGHBOURING VILLAGES AND TOWNS.

I visited Bayou la Fourche, Huma, Barataria-Bay, Thibodeaux, Franklin. [Page 47] Donaldsonville. St. Martins, Jackson, La., (where I became acquainted with Major Dunn and family,) Vermonville, Opelousa, Bayou Playquemine, Point Coupee, St. Francisville, Point Hudson, Baton Rouge, Lafeyette, Algiers, &c., thus making myself acquainted with the people and country. Also visited Madison across lake Ponchartrain, and I really must not forget my kind old friend, Mr. Bell, who kept the Washington Hotel on the Ponchartrain Lake; who always made me at home in his own pleasant house. Also I cheerfully tender my humble thanks to the directors of the Ponchartrain and Nashville railroad; also the Carrolton railroad who have all acted a brotherly part towards me. Also the captains and crews of various steamers. In this pleasant manner Autumn and Winter came and passed, and in the Spring as I had been pretty regular at my business, I easily obtained permission to take a little trip up the Mississippi. I had often been invited to Nashville, Ten., and now determined to go and pay the place a visit. I accordingly took some cigars and candy, and a few of my instruments, and went aboard Capt. John Russell's boat, who went, however, only as far as Memphis; then went aboard the Cumberland, (The Captain's name I am sorry to say have forgotten.) The boat was heavily laden and a large number of passengers were on board of her. All was pleasant and quiet; sold all my cigars at the bar of the boat. In order to give the keeper of the bar a little respite. I had attended to his affairs for one day. At night after the captain and passengers had all retired, the boat being just at the mouth of the Cumberland river, all at once the boat trembled and stopped short as if some mighty hand had arrested her progress. The roof fell in, the partitions were broken down, the drawers were dislodged from their places, and the passengers from their berths, some were almost frightened out of their senses. Ladies were running in all directions, some screaming, some praying, while now and then came deep groans from some one greatly distressed. All was confusion. It was soon ascertained that a large snag had passed through the boat about midway, forcing its way through the captains's berth where he was asleep, injuring his spine so much that his recovery was deemed hopeless. The boat seemed fast filling with water.—The skiff was loosed and filled with passengers. Many jumped overboard and swam ashore; some who could swim well, taking with them some poor helpless female; for those who were left were nearly frantic with fear. I by chance got hold of the planks used in forming the stage to bring freight aboard. I told them that I thought I could manage to get two of them ashore; immediately three of them [Page 48] jumped in and were clinging to the plank. I succeeded in getting them safe to the shore and then went back to the boat. But they had found that the snag could be taken out, which was done, and the hole partially stopped and the boat carefully and quickly steered to the shore. I then assisted to search out the skiff. They had left the oars and had floated on to a sand bar where they were awaiting day light, from whence we took them to Smithland where we all succeeded in getting quarters. The most of the lives and property were saved, and it certainly might have been much worse, but to see, as I saw my fellow mortals begging for help, was a scene I never wish to witness again.

This completely turned my mind from Nashville, and I went with Captain Montgomery up the Ohio. I however changed boats several times at Cincinnati and Wheeling, I believe. I visited the band in Pittsburg. My acquaintance was somewhat limited. Having sold out, I took stage across the country to Cleveland, Ohio. While at Cleveland, I visited the Sandusky Indians. From Cleveland I went to Painesville and Chardon; and returning to Cleveland, sailed to Detroit. I then started homeward by way of Columbus, Dayton, and Cincinnati. At Cincinnati I became acquainted with Captain Summons and family. I reached home in safety, and was ever glad to get home and see my old friends.

I made frequent excursions during the last years of my stay in New Orleans. On one occasion I took passage on board the steamer George Washington, Mr. Egerton, Captain. And I take the liberty of saying that he was on the eve of being married to the accomplished Miss Catherine Oldham, of Louisville, Ky. I was introduced to the family, and many of the first families of that city. The day for the marriage to take place was fixed, and I played now and then for the Captain and his lady love, to while away the time, which seemed to hang heavy on their hands; but the wedding day at length arrived, and a bright affair it was too; afterwards they went down to the George Washington and had a ball; here my music was just the thing. During this time I saw the Hon. Henry Clay, for the first time. I knew nothing of politics, but I was much pleased with the man himself. I went to a convention of the whig party; Mr. Clay was the hero of the day. I often played at different political gatherings, without distinction of party.

I visited Bay St. Louis and was welcomed by the citizens. When I visited a city I was lucky enough to find those whom I could esteem as friends, by playing some of their favorite melodies. Thus wherever I [Page 49] roamed, with this unseen key did I unlock the heart of the stranger, and find the priceless treasure of a friend. O, where and what should I have been, had not nature planted within me this clue to that changeable organ, the human heart! With it I could disarm envy, avert the eye of suspicion, and although not able, even yet, to clip the tongue of scandal, yet have I trudged side by side with it, and gained more friends than it could make me enemies. When I returned, all of my acquaintances were very glad to see me; it was near the hour for reviewing, and as I was riding through the city, I met a carriage full of friends, who being the first people of the United States, were at liberty to act as to them seemed best, without the fear of enemies; they alighted from their carriage, and crowned me with a wreath of flowers, thus testifying their regard for me in honor of my uncultivated talents. This touched a tender chord in my bosom, and I mentally exclaimed, what am I? As I remembered the crown of thorns, it melted me even unto tears, and I feared that I had murmured withal; a strange foreboding crept into my heart, and I felt to resign myself into the hands of God, with confidence to believe that he in his own time would deliver me from this dreadful uncertainty.

AN EVENTFUL VISIT AMONG THE CREEKS AND SEMINOLES, OR THE FLORIDA INDIANS, ABOUT THE CLOSE OF THE MEMORABLE FLORIDA WAR.

There was much said at this time that excited my compassion for the Indians of that country. I felt that they would at length be over-powered, insomuch that they would be obliged to remove to the far West, or suffer themselves to be exterminated. I knew that they abhorred the very idea of removing from their hunting-ground which they considered theirs only. Their forefathers had held undisputed sway there, for many thousand moons. There they had lived, and there they had died, bequeathing their all to their children, which they left behind them. Those simple children of the woods were content with their lot, and had not sought to enrich themselves in any wise, but were satisfied to live as their forefathers had lived, and die as they had died, without name or knowledge to extend beyond the limits of their own tribe, except their traditions and predilections. But when their removal was insisted upon, the very demon of evil seemed to have taken possession of their hearts, destroying in his dangerous course [Page 50] every feeling of a gentle or friendly nature. I was somewhat acquainted with some of those with whom they were contending. I had had an opportunity of associating with the whites from childhood. I foresaw that they were determined, and would never surrender, or in other words, give up the chase until the Indian was no longer an inhabitant of that soil. I heard even my own friends condemn the poor Indian for trying to defend what he believed to be his, and his alone. Would not my friends do the same? Yes, more. Oh, why do we mortals ever look upon our enemies' faults through magnifying glasses! As I pondered these things over again and again, a secret desire to visit that tribe soon had grown into a resolute determination, to use my endeavours to show them the hopelessness of their efforts—to impress upon their minds that at the most they would only have blood and revenge, for the blood of their kindred; and in the end, shame and disgrace, and the loss of their lands besides. Full of these feelings I set out for Florida. I had scarce ever felt more solemnity on my mind at any other period of my chequered existence. When once there my plan was not so easily put into execution. I found that the least word in favor of removal was dangerous to the peace and life of the individual who dared to give utterance to such counsel, and still claim to be the Indian's friend, Such I claimed to be, and felt that I really was. I could make myself understood in French and Spanish, as some of them spoke a little of each language. I had said nothing of my name or blood, but ventured a few suggestions to them, which I soon learned had caused all to regard me with an unfriendly and suspicious eye. I felt ill at ease in my own mind at first, but then I reflected on the purity of my motives, and determined to hide all traces of such feelings; to mix in their company boldly and fearlessly, trusting the event with God, believing he would open the way to their hearts, though they were now filled with the deadly passions of hatred and strife; that they would yet be able to understand and appreciate my motives.

INDIAN BURIAL.

The warriors were preparing to bury one of their number. It was indeed a solemn scene. The wail of the women in mourning, ever and anon reached my ears. At length the body was taken, and all his blankets and war equipments, his gun, tomahawk, scalping-knife, &c., [Page 51] with many things which designated his honorable achievements. All was silent as the grave itself, while the funeral ceremonies were performing. He was then wrapped in his blankets and borne to his grave. He had many friends, and was deeply mourned; and then the impending trouble,—the grief of the whole nation served to heighten the solemnity of the occasion. Many people were gathered together to follow him to his final resting spot; but before the ceremonies were concluded, many of the women cast themselves upon the ground, as if they wished thus to give publicity to the hopelessness of their grief, and the despair which had as it were taken full possession of their souls. As the corpse was borne away, the sound of their wild lamentations as it gushed forth from their stricken hearts, fell heavily on the ear, carrying sadness to the liveliest bosom in the ranks. When they arrived at the grave, some of the wives of the warriors and maidens were still in the ranks. The people were prepared to perform the last office, to pay the last tribute of respect, and fulfil the last duty, in the consignment of the mortal remains of their friend and brother to their destined and final abode. Some of the women were kneeling, covering their faces with their hands weeping most bitterly, while others lay extended and disconsolate upon the ground, seemingly impressed with grief too overpowering to be expressed.

The men turned from each other for a moment, as they seemed silently consulting the Great Spirit in the chamber of their own hearts; some leaning against trees, others on their guns, while some had unstrung their bows and placed one end on the ground, supporting the other in the hand, at the

same time suffering the head to droop listlessly there, while some were engaged in placing the body in the right position. Nothing could exceed the
precious care with which each article was consigned to its respective place.
Then they one and all seemed to arouse from the stupor of grief and went
through with the ceremony of taking leave of the dead. The men all locking
their hands behind their heads and walking off, and the women uniting in
a kind of funeral dirge retired from the grave.

HOW INDIANS ACQUIRE THEIR NAMES.

When we were preparing to return to our homes, temporary as they really were, I found I had several friends here, although I was unconscious of the presence of any, save Chief Walker and Lightfoot. Then [Page 52] stepped forth a man called Chief Alligator. This curious name was given him from the following circumstances;—

He having unexpectedly started out hunting one morning, found out that he had neglected to supply himself with bullets for the day. He had used the last one, and was returning home, when a track arrested his attention, and he carelessly followed it along merely to see where it might go, and he became engaged, and ere he was aware, had advanced into the swamp. He stopped, wishing in the meantime he could proceed, and yet he was conscious that his best way was the back track. As he thus stood, he observed an alligator making more than common speed towards him, from the direction in which he had entered; but a little way before him lay some old logs, towards which he made his way, yet doubtful how affairs would turn, for his enemy was close in pursuit, and he was without his accustomed means of defence.

The logs proved to be lying on a bank of a bayou of the Mississippi. He climbed over them, but his foe though unwieldly in his proportions, was close at his heels. The Indian knew by his movements that he was oppressed with hunger and consequently would attack him. He was a monster, the largest of his kind, and light defence seemed likely to aggravate and rouse him to anger, rather than to stay him from his purpose. The Indian quickly tore a branch from an old tree, broke it a little shorter than what he supposed to be the width of the animal's mouth when open; he then stretched himself full length on the log, shut his eyes, and pretented to sleep soundly. His enemy approached, and as he had hoped, placed his jaws close to the log, and opened his mouth; no sooner did the Indian hear that, than he jammed into it the stick he held. Thus as the animal endeavored to seize upon him, he propped his mouth wide open, which entirely disarmed his opponent, who rolled and pitched—snorted with anger, settling the stick, (which the Indian had pointed at each end) far into his jaws, which now seemed to cause him great pain; but he could not extricate himself therefrom. It was now the Indian's turn. He fought his monster enemy until he was just on the brink of the water. He had wearied himself from his own exertions so much, that the Indian pushed him into the water, and easily drowned him. He saved and sold the oil, which amply paid him for his time and trouble; so to use the Indian's own words, "he caught the Alligator napping, and beat him at his own game." He tells the story, then adds, "Me! when you see me sleep, you look sharp; eyes shut, then me wide awake: ears open, me hear all you say, see all you do; if eyes [Page 53] open, then me fast asleep heap; ears shut, me no hear, me no see; do all you like, me no know it." So they called him sleeping Alligator; a fine noble fellow he was too. We were happy in each other's friendship, and I was truly glad to find him here. There was also a Creek Chief here, with whom I had a slight acquaintance; but who went altogether by his Indian name. I have forgotten the exact pronunciation, though I have by no means forgotten my friend. Some of the red men and pale faced names have slipped my memory, as I could not write, and never really thought of having even the outlines of my life written down. I only kept the memorandum in my head. I know the Chief of whom I have last spoken, had a sister married to a white man, whose name I believe was Walker.

RECOGNIZED BY PUCH-CHEE-NUBBEE, AN OLD ACQUAINTANCE OF MY FATHER.—A THRILLING HISTORY GIVEN OF THE FATE OF MY NATION THE CHOCTAWS.

As the man of years came forward, whose name was Puch Chee-Nubbee, he was received with the cordiality to which an unstained and honourable old age is entitled to in civilized society. I noticed his eye fell on me, while an unusual degree of anxious inquiry seemed to accompany the penetrating glance. I felt that he was searching my very heart, and a child-like sympathy agitated my bosom; years of sorrow rolled on before me. O! how I wished that I could fall upon the neck that supported that venerable head and call him my father! I moved not. All was silent. He stepped a few paces nearer and said—"young stranger, I have seen you but little, yet I must know more of you. Do you like the company of the aged, who stand like the noble tree over whose head the tempest of an hundred years has broken, stripping it of branches and beauty, yet unable to uproot its strength?" I answered him when he ceased to speak, by saying, that the reality of the picture he had just drawn, always reminded me of old age, and that I could not express my love for aged and gray-haired men. He seemed affected, not so much by my words, as by the thoughts that were passing in his own mind. He asked me to go with him to his camp;—I readily assented. By his request the others accompanied us. The utmost silence was maintained. I thought I had felt very solemn in the march behind the dead. Yet I must confess that my feelings were a little changed, though the day was far spent, ere we were safely lodged within the old man's camp. [Page 54] He motioned us to be seated. He spoke to his companions at the same time in his own tongue. I would have given much to have known exactly what he was then saying. All eyes turned anxiously upon me at the same time, which left no doubt but that he had been speaking of me. Being conscious that I had offended some of the tribe, in endeavouring to offer consolation, and advising them to make peace, I scarcely knew what result to expect; I did not know what to say, that is, what I could say to the purpose, and so concluded I would wait in silence, the pleasure of my host. But I was not kept long in suspense; for as soon as all was still he turned to me and said: "Young man, I want you to show us your right foot, you do it?" "Certainly" I replied, and with all possible haste laid my foot bare to their observation. The old man lifted his clasped hands, raised his eyes to wards heaven, and said: "Me, I know him. His father good Choctaw chief; Me I see that," pointing to my right foot, "Me see him fall." Then seeming suddenly to recollect himself, he looked at me and said, "young man, our ears are unstopped, speak, we will hear you talk of your father." I relieved my aching heart with a deep drawn sigh, and answered, "let my aged father speak on; I am a child; I have had no parents to teach me how to speak. My words lack wisdom, and I am ashamed to say I never knew my father." He answered, "And your mother died ere you knew how to keep her memory in your mind. Your father one good man, Great Choctaw Chief. He live on Tombigbee river; his home on Dancing Rabbit Creek. Pushmataha, Mosholeh Tubbee, and Laflour took some men to go to big white house to see their white father. Pale-face want more lands, no got enough; Indian got little spot, Pale-face want it bad.

Indian all sorry; all say no, no; Mosholeh Tubbee say no; Laflour very mad; when pale-face camp came, said we must make treaty. We no go home, no when treaty made, then we go. Pale-face neighbors all round hate Indians; he better go; bad pale-face kill him. Chiefs call the people together; all say no, we cannot go; we cannot leave our homes; they hold the bones of our fathers, we cannot leave them. All very angry; Laflour, he mad plenty; he say, bad pale-face! all bad! no good, I no like him; he got many lands, no children on all his lands; he came here many moons ago, he very good, he say Great Spirit speak and send him to poor Indian to teach him to wor-ship the Great Spirit better; say our fathers no worship him right; they no know how. He came within our wigwam; warmed himself by our fire; ate of our salt; said he was our freind. We believed him. We made him welcome. [Page 55] Many of us received his religion; he was very glad, very happy. Then he bring his people, who soon want all our lands; drive Indian off. He offer us nasty swamps, where we cannot live; he want us to die, We no go; he no have our land; brothers, he no have it! When I make treaty, I tell you, you cut of my head. The people all say they have no treaty. They break up, go home; all glad again. Pale-face coax Indian chiefs to come there in their camp; by and by make friends; he give fire water plenty; chiefs go back, feel very good; pale face very good; fire water burn up all poor Indian's sense; make him very bad man, very bad chief; forget poor people. Pale-face say, come now, write your names here, then all you want you have. We your friends; make big wish, you have it; your white father says so; send us here to give you plenty.

"'Twas dark midnight; the good spirits had all left the earth; the Indians' hearts were dark; there was no light in them, but fire water. The pale-face held the pen in the Indian's hand, guiding it until their names were written. They wished; Mosholeh Tubbee wished one big pile of gold money, and one gold measure of the sun (watch); Laflour one silver fine carriage, such as the big men at the white house; plenty money too. When morning came, and the good spirits returned on the rays of the morning sun, then they were very sorry: they go and say pale-face, give me back my word, and take these monies; I have ruined my people But pale-face laughed; he no give it back, he too glad. Then chiefs very shamed, very sorry, they no want coun-cil. Their people hear, they no believe; they hear again and again, then they believe, then they mourn and lament. They no fight like our brothers here; they bowed their heads in deep sorrow, and called their people together to listen, while they talked.

We all signified a desire to hear more, as the old man concluded by saying. I remember many of their words. He began by saying, the Choctaw Chief said, "I am glad so many of you have come to sit, for the last time where our forefathers sat; are your ears open to hear the words of your counsellors? for here our council fire blazed high many, many moons ago; here our forefathers lit and smoked the pipe of peace with my friends. Not only the pipe was lit here by them, but the heart was warmed up with kindly feelings for their own people, and their pale-faced friends were not forgotten: for we have ever been friends. Not the blood of the pale-face can be found with the Choctaw; but our warriors have numbered with him in his battles; for this, other tribes have [Page 56] hated us, and called us women, who loved the pale-face more than their own race. But he was the friend of our forefathers of whom we have just spoken; they are shades, yet their ears are not shut; but they hear and pity their children; and now while we are here, the wind which we feel on our cheeks is their breath, and the gentle mist before the heavy rain, yes, and the bright dew drops kiss them up, for it is their tears. A stranger might wonder why they are shed, but ye already know. Ye know that the pale-faces foot hath been among us and left its print here; we know that soon after he came to us, he said he came a messenger of peace from the Great Spirit; that we did not worship him well, consequently he was not pleased with us, and sent him to teach us to worship him better. He said he was our friend; and could we do less than to warm him and give him meat? His words were good; his councils were great; we loved him. Many of us have received his religion, who do not yet return. His brethern came and dwelt near us, teaching us many things; but no sooner had he done exulting in the succesful accomplishment of his plans, than he (shall I say he?) O! was it he, or his brother, that begrudged us our homes here on the loved Mississippi: brothers was not the pale face honest, but his eyes are large. Not satisfied with the broad lands on the shores of the Atlantic, and great lakes and rivers, which the Indian has relinquished as he was driven back step by step; yes, in many of their former homes there is not scarce a wigwam remaining to send forth its smoke to the sun upon the breath of the Great Spirit. No, they have travelled westward, though they sometimes journey there to visit the former hunting grounds and burial places of their forefathers. Does this unsatisfied appetite arise in man from that civilization which we have invited among us? it is through that source? We have hoped that feelings of a different nature should arise from this source. O, Great Spirit, hast thou forsaken us, or art thou angry that we have forsaken the worship of our fathers, and turned ourselves to strangers! Our possessions here have become very small, yet they are not the less dear, and we had hoped to keep this little spot; but the pale-face asked for it; we have said no, no; talked until we are weary, but their ears are shut, they hear not our word, and the great white father has even demanded it of us; what remains to be done? He is stronger than we, and he is our forefathers' friend. The lands which they offer, seem to us but miry swamps, where our nation will survive but a few years at the farthest. Should we leave these lands, where, O! where, should [Page 57] we find a spot to rest our weary feet. It is hard but we cannot resist; he is stronger than we, and our fathers' friend. What remains to be done but to call our women and children together and prepare for the departure. Let us nerve up and strengthen the heart; to say to them that we are exiles without friends or home, save the wilds of the forest. There we are offered a resting spot forever; as long as grass shall grow, and water run. O, pale-face, dost thou speak with a forked tongue that has deceived many of our fathers and brothers. Ye will crowd us out of homes, and the last look which we cast behind us, though our eyes would fain look forever on those loved homes; yet, that last look shall be short, and the pale-face will say, as he ever says, "The Indian cannot feel." But we appeal to thee, O! Great Spirit! thou knowest us better, and we pray thee to judge between us. And you, ye Cypress trees, bend lower down and touch our foreheads with your friendly branches; pity us that we are irrevocably doomed to bid thee an eternal farewell, though we have loved you from childhood. Many of us when first conscious of life, found ourselves cradled on your limbs, and rocked by the breath of the Great Spirit as he breathed blessings upon their young heads, while the mother sat employed below. Perhaps that mother sleeps that awful sleep of dust returning to its mother dust, near or on that very spot, causing it to be still more sacred and doubly dear. And now to the pale-face we say, see that ye worship the Great Spirit well, lest he avenge our unmerited wrongs on your heads, for you have caused us to drink of the bitter cup. Ye have not offered sweetening, but have said, drain the dregs. We say beware; we go yet not willingly but in peace; beware lest the Great Spirit order you or your children to drink it all again. Beware! we go! we go! we go!" Then continued the old man, my heart was very weak. I listened to these words and many more. Yes, I saw and heard them invoke the spirits of their dead to forgive them that their bones should be left behind; to accuse them not, though the burial ground of the Indian family became the garden spot of the white man. Yes, with up-lifted hands they besought them for strength to perform the painful duties which had fallen to their lot; that they might visit for the last time, the sacred spot where they had borne their bodies, when their spirits sought the peaceful hunting grounds of the Spirit land, where they can build their wigwam, and spread their blankets down in peace, and fear no enemies, nor dread their removal. They called for strength to tear the dear images of their long cherised homes from their lacerated hearts, promising [Page 58] at the same time that the wound should never heal, that the vacancy should never be filled; that no other spot should ever be half so dear as their own loved homes; that they should ever be strangers; that they would welcome death when he came, that they might then join their forefathers, and be at home. Then said thy father (speaking to me) in those days of bitter sorrow, "O my son, do I leave thy bones here in these lands. Has the panther, bear, or the wolf, robbed me of thee, thou child of promise to a fond father; or has some of the enemies of my tribe stolen thee from me when thy father's face was turned from thee. O, better were it for thee poor child, to have met the deadly embrace of the beast of prey, than thy fine limbs should be sub-jected to the blows of strangers. There are those of my own race who hate me because I have been a friend to the pale face, and my heart is maddened at the thought, lest thou shouldst now writhe under the iron hand of slav-ery in some other tribe, perhaps, or in the settlements of the whites. Thou hast, if still alive, outgrown all thy father's memory of thy infantile features; yet there are marks on thee that thy friends could not mistake. Well for thy gentle mother that she never knew thy fate. Or perhaps she looked down from the Spirit-land and welcomed the spirit of her adored child to her longing embrace, and introduced the spirit of the young chief to the de-parted chiefs and warriors of the tribe of his fathers. O! could I but know this, my heart would be at rest; for I shall soon join them all, and visit those friends from whom I have been so long separated; but something ever whispers me, he is here yet. I can so plainly see his face and form, even yet, and feel that he is in sorrow! for in my dreams he comes to me so lifelike, though sorrowful, I at times feel that I cannot mistake."

PATRIARCHAL CUSTOM OF BLESSING CHILDREN, OBSERVED BY THE INDIANS.

Then I call to mind the words of the wise man of my tribe, who blessed him and pronounced him long life and wisdom, to exceed even that of his ancestors; that his judgment should be highly prized by the people; and his company and counsel sought by the counsellers of his tribe; that he should have wisdom to detect the false-hearted, and expose his wickedness, and a kind heart to relieve the oppressed; judgment to administer relief to the afflicted; that the beggar should not ask of him in vain for food, or the weary one for rest; this said he and still more. [Page 59] When I call to mind the feelings of my own heart as we repaired to the water, to test the truth or falsehood of the old man's words, and to see if the Great Spirit would accept the babe, and bless him according to the old man's words; we took the ice from the pure stream, and as his infant form was laid into the cold water, my heart seemed to have ceased to beat, suspense had checked it. I gasped for breath, that I might see my little idol left to sink or swim, to live or die; but he passed the ordeal in safety, lightly floating on the bright water. I received him into my arms, and secretly pressed him to my bosom, vowing within, that all my renown, the honor of all my achievments, and a large portion of my possessions should be transmitted to this child of my love. Then again I received him from the arms of his dying mother, my young and tender wife. In that hour of bitterness, grief and separation, I promised to love the child she had given me more than all things else on the earth; that as he had been the darling of our hearts, on whose head our love and future hopes had concentrated, so in her absence I would idolize him, with a two-fold affection, that through the child, the mother, though absent from the earth, though withdrawn from the sight of the mortal vision, yet through this means she should hold communication with my heart, that she could thus be present to the eyes of my inner sight. That while I looked on the child, she should continue to live in my heart. Ah! but too faithfully have I discharged that obligation. For a while I was so intent upon keeping and minutely fulfilling that promise, so jealous was I of my charge, that I carried him in my arms by day, and slept with him there at night. The tender mother's ready eye would have been less vigilant than mine. Would to heaven that I had suffered him to emerge into manhood while yet borne in a father's arms. Had I suffered the young to gain its strength thus, I had now been cheerful and happy, where now this heart is weary and stricken with the weight of cares and blighted hopes. But the evil spirit prevailed against me, in an unguarded hour. I left him but for a few days at most; but he was doomed, and I was too proud to hear all who saw him, speak in his praise; and then to hear my friends so often congratulate me that my playful child so much resembled his father; and yet I had trusted him from my sight but a few hours, ere all my hopes were crushed by his loss. The news reached me ere three days. I was stung to the heart, maddened with grief. The pale pace had been to our place to trade with us, but was now gone. I called my brothers together. Accustomed as the red man is from his [Page 60] earliest infancy onward to the grave, to hide all outward signs of emotion from the human eye; though the heart-strings are strained with sorrow ready to bursting, yet the same calm exterior must be preserved; my brothers reprimanded me for being overwhelmed with sorrow which knew no bounds. They maintained there was still hope of his recovery; they offered me their assistance, promising to watch closely the enemies of our tribe, for some contended they had stolen him. The pale face route was intersected, and they were closely questioned and narrowly watched, but without success. They had answered all questions with much apparent candour; said they had not the child; which was plainly evident. Then one of their number recollected that two of them were missing; on being interrogated they frankly confessed the truth; yet the spies were apprehensive that a slight shadow of embarrassment was visible on their countenances. After a moment's silence, they of their own free will explained, when, where, and why, they had left them; spoke freely of their business, and pointed out the route they had taken, and explained that they had gone thither to purchase cattle; which seemed very probable.

It was a journey of two or three days and nights before we could reach the place designated; and when we arrived, there were no such people there, neither had there been. Judge of the state of my mind on finding this to be the case. I felt that we were duped, and that the men and child were hid when we were there. I now reflected on myself that I had not offered all which I possessed as a ransom for my child. We retraced our footsteps, but gloom still more terrible seemed to gather round. I had left some trusty hearts to watch unseen, the proceedings of the pale face traders, when I found what they had told us had not even the shadow of truth in it. All my hope was that he was concealed, and would be found out by my spies. Such was my state of mind, that anxiety seemed to have entirely rooted the feeling of revenge out of my heart, and I determined to doubly reward any one who would return my child, or even bring tidings of him, let them be good or bad. I found that grief, fatigue, and hunger, were upon me, for indeed I had given way to hope and fear, grief and despair.

Suffering from the most intense anxiety, the stricken father trembled like a frightened fawn, as he approached his home. There my hopes were doomed to wither and die, as the summer flower before the chilling breath of an autumnal frost. Ah! how often have I asked myself, will their spring ever return?—will they ever bloom more? or had their [Page 61] atmosphere turned to one unchanging winter, and ceaseless storm, and endless night! My people had secretly watched the traders by day and night, following in their train when they were far from place, and indeed until they had left my lands; they had not yet returned. My poor comrades were worn with the fatigue and hardships of so constantly riding. They begged me to take some repose, and then asked for one night's rest for themselves and beasts. How could I refuse or urge them further? I could not wear out the living, for one whom I feared was dead to me.

My scouts returned; they were satisfied that no child was with them; their comrades had not joined them as yet, neither could they find that they expected them. They had betrayed no signs of uneasiness. I now began to fear that the child had been suffered to stray too far away, and some wild beast had devoured him. Or perhaps the evil spirit had thus avenged himself of us, because we had ceased to make offerings to him, or endeavoured to do anything to appease his anger; but had trusted altogether to the Spirit of good, regardless of his anger. I knew that some of the tribes still offered sacrifice to him, and I reasoned, had not he given my child into the hands of his followers, who hated us because we were friendly with the pale face, to whom they were enemies; consequently they were enemies to us. Had he not given up my child to die, ere he knew how to die; or perhaps they would chose to let him live, and teach him to hate his own tribe; to hear him speak evil of his own father's name, while that father was secretly indulging in hopeless grief for his irreparable loss of his son. We rode over a great portion of the Indian land, making secretly all the observations possible; also making many inquiries which tended to the one great aim of my life. My friends advised me to endeavor to lock up my grief in my heart. Trusting that if the child lived, he might be offered for a ransom; thinking that if he had been stolen, when all signs of grief and resentment had passed away they would seek to return him for money. I accordingly instructed all my friends to pay liberally for the least intelligence; to give lavishly to any one who gave the least information that seemed at all to the point; though they were sure the bearer of the tidings for which they were paying, had the child in his possession, yet they should not seem to dream of such a thing being possible, and only exhibit the most anxious solicitude for the return of the lost child to his father's arms.

[Page 62] THE WISE MAN CONSULTED.

My heart was in darkness, and so the light of hope was for a time, shut out. I had rode much, and was weary in body and mind. I at length sought the dwelling of my old friend, the wise man of my people, I had sent a messenger to acquaint him of my loss, my grief, and apprise him of my intended visit to his place, to receive his counsel and instruction. Now that I had come, he received me in a spirit of extreme kindness, yet he did not at first break the sad silence, with aught save the language of his eyes, as he fixed a sorrowful look upon me. I trembled with emotion too power- ful for utterance. I read in his compassionate and brotherly glance, that he pitied me from the inmost chambers of his soul; for he too, had loved and blessed the child. He at length observed, "My brother's heart is dark; the sun has not shone there for many days; dark clouds have gathered thickly about his head; his eyes cannot see for the water thereof; are his ears open? if so, it is well; we will spend the day together, and when you have taken some necessary repose, I would propose that we repair to the mountain, the dwelling-place of the Great Spirit." He wished me to take some rest. I insisted that I neither needed or desired rest, nor yet was able to take it, it being altogether out of my reach. I soon saw that I must at least endeavor to obey and respect his kind wishes; and at length suffered him to persuade me to seek sleep. I laid me down with as much composure as possible, just to please the aged man whose guest I was. He seemed quite pleased with my acquiescence and apparent resignation. He set about preparing me a draught of tea, which I had scarcely taken and listened to the instruc- tive discourses, and soothing words of my friend, who gradually drew my mind away from its theme of sorrow, when ere I was aware of the same, the sweet and soothing sensations of sleep were stealing over my weary frame. I gradually resigned myself into its friendly arms, as I still yet listened to the old man's voice, as it gently lulled my spirit into heartfelt security; as it seemed to die away in the distance, and I heard it only as the faint murmurings of the limpid water, as I, while yet an untroubled child, laid me down on the shady banks of the stream listening to the language of the water, the sighing of the summer wind, until I ceased to remember that I was a living being. Though it was scarce yet mid-day, yet morning had dawned ere I awoke again to consciousness.

[Page 63] SINGULAR CUSTOM OF GOING UPON THE MOUNTAIN TO CONSULT THE GREAT SPIRIT.

The preparations for our journey were ready made, and ere long we were under way. He told me had prayed much for me since he heard of my trouble, and that now we were going where no evil had ever been able to survive; that as soon as they come near the sacred spot, the thunderings from the voice of the Great Spirit, the fire which proceeded out of his mouth, as his anger arose, because of the wicked ways of the tribes of men, who were the children of the earth which he held as his own; also because of the evil doings of the evil spirits which wandered through the earth destroying its loveliness, and sadly changing the face thereof; so much so, that when he chose to visit through the earth, his holiness was so much shocked, and so highly incensed, that he took up his abode in the mountain, consecrating the spot sacred forever to his holiness. Here he established the throne of the thunders; that may dwell for ever issuing forth their deep voices, where the lightnings sport in playful gambols; the very sky reflecting back its fiery and zig-zag forms, immediately annihilating anything of an evil nature, which had the misfortune to approach within the limits of the sacred dwelling. That the great Spirit had been so kind as to establish good and benovelent Spirits to guard the earth and her children from the depredations of the evil ones, who seek only to destroy the beauty of the earth; the good designs of the children of men, whose eyes they blind with the mists of sorrow, and whose cares are rendered entirely deaf to the voice of the spirits of good, because they are continually filled with the lying whispers of those evil spirits, and cannot discern the voice of the good spirit who would be their friend and give comforting and instructive council, to soothe the troubled spirit by promising a peaceful home in the pleasant hunting-grounds of the Spirit land, where our fore-fathers luxuriate in the blessings and beauty of one eternal spring.

On arriving at the foot of the mountain, we prepared to ascend its rugged side together. We proceeded some way in silence; my heart could not but admire the stupendous grandeur of the scene below. My companion acted as guide; for he was not like me a stranger on this hallowed ground; he had there sought council from the Holy Spirit before. At length he halted, and I could but regard him with a kind of religious awe, as he pointed out a spot where I could rest; observing that he wished to ascend farther into the mountains. I felt that he [Page 64] certainly must doubt my ability to proceed. I was desirous to proceed, yet was as passive as a child in the hands of his father. I made no objection, but readily assented to his proposal. Never had my spirit been so humbled, so subdued, as at present time. The conversation of the day, the solemn beauty of the spot, the precarious and melancholy state of my mind, and the excitement under which I had labored for many weeks; all together served to work my mind up to that degree, that I seemed to hear the whispers of the Great Spirit mingling in with the sighs of the wind which lingered in the mountain. On being left alone, in a spot too, which I felt I had no just cause to consider less than holy, with feelings which I cannot describe, I bowed myself to the earth. It was not exactly despair which took possession of me, but rather deep and hopeless grief; for that keen conviction had returned with two-fold acuteness that my child still lived; and that very conviction seemed to bend my spirit still lower, that he should live and still I was unable to trace out the place of his concealment; to tear asunder his unhallowed bonds, was a thought almost unendurable to a father who was otherwise stricken and bereaved by the hand of death, who never seeks or even wishes to repay the loss you sustain; the deep wounds which he ungenerously inflicts without leave or ceremony, perfectly regardless of the virtue, wealth, fame, or beauty, of the object chosen for its prey. I almost breathlessly awaited the return of my good friend, whom I now more anxiously desired to see, than at any other period of my life. A kind of a vague realizing sense of what he would say, seemed to be impressed upon me. When he returned, he seated himself near where I lay, and when I looked on him, he motioned me to rise from that prostrate position. I scarce had strength to obey, so prostrate were my energies of body and mind. I did not speak, but he seeming conscious of my disposition to do so, but lacked the strength; he kindly assisted me, seating himself on my side, regarding me steadily in the eye, as if he expected me to speak; but I chose to leave it altogether to his own pleasure to break the silence; for in truth, I knew not what to say. This he did in a few moments by saying: "Great and good Chief of a noble race, mourn not without hope; forget not those who look up to thee for council to guide them. Who shall fill thy place to them when thou art gone? Forsake them not, while the Great Spirit guards thy sojourn among his people; ere long, and the spirits of our forefathers will call for thee into the lands of the shades, and then thy people will mourn for thee. Rouse thee up; cause them not to mourn ere the [Page 65] time; let them not mourn while thou art still present with them, lest the shades of thy fathers should say, he is not worthy of his charge, and should be grieved at so shameful a thought. Forsake them not in their grief, but be comforted. My brother, let us reason together. Have we not known instances where birds were decoyed and ensnared when they were young, and kept from enjoying liberty, so sweet to all things when young; and when they were middle aged, liaving obtained that freedom for which they have ever sighed, have they not flown higher, and longer, in their ecstacies; ventured farther, risked more, than those who have had a long life of practice; just because it was new to them, and then so sweet that they thought not of dangers, but soared on in triumph, consequently passing through unmultiplied dangers in safety and pleasure. Now listen to me. I lie not. My words are spoken in truth; they are the words of an aged man who is your friend. The dark clouds of a wintry storm have gathered about the head of the Chief, and the angry blasts of pitiless winds of adversity have blown away, no one knows whither, the idol of his heart, where all hopes, his heart's best affections. were enshrined. He groans under the pressure of the iron hand of bitterness and sorrow, which, panther-like, suddenly, yet effectively, seized upon his heart which lay secure as the speckled fawn trusting to its mother's vigilant eye for its security and life; but it is crushed with a demon's grasp; yet it writhes and flutters in hopeless agony, yet eagerly watching an opportunity to make its escape.

Receive this thy sorrow as becometh one of a noble race. Bear up under thy loss as becometh a man of experience, and receive it as a forerunner of the complicated sorrows which await thy tribe; for they will change their ways more and more. The pale-face has spoken to them with a forked tongue; many who profess friendship will prove their enemies; for they will secretly lay plans to undermine the Indian; to strip him of his foot-hold here. They will ask for these lands. The people will laugh that they should suppose they would leave the land where their fathers slept. The white man will press them still more, but the people will angrily answer, No! no! then he who once called himself our brother, but has now usurped a father's authority over us, will demand it. The people will with one voice cry, No! Yet their voice will reach no ears; all are shut to the wail of their mourning; their claims will fade away, and like the morning dew, cannot be found when the sun gained his noonday height and splendor. Then will many hearts be desolate as thine, and the child shall cling to the mother who has no [Page 66] home to shelter its tender limbs. They shall go sorrowing and mourning to a far-off land, where many will sicken and die, for their hearts will break. They will remember that they were crowded unwillingly away from homes sacredly dear, and while the fire which they left on the hearths of their homes is still alive, the pale face will rush in, casting about him an eagle's glance, betraying at once that his avaricious heart is unsatisfied that no greater treasures are left behind. But the good pale face* will go with him; he will not forsake them, but will humbly endeavor to comfort them in their day of affliction; to give the light of hope to all who will receive. Then they will live where and as the Indian lives; he will suffer when they suffer, and rejoice in their joy; and he will die where the Indian dies, and lay his bones in their new home. They will assume the habits of the pale face, and the tribe will begin to prosper. The days of their sorrow shall have an end, and their joy shall be crowned with peace; they will increase in number again, and abundance shall be the blessing and fruit of their labors. They will prosper and become happier than the red man has been since the first great canoe of the pale face landed on the distant shores of the land of the red man. Since that day all the visions of the Indians have been clouded with ill. As the oppressed with drooping spirits and crushed hearts, relinquished to the oppressor the last claim which he had to the beautiful land of his youthful adventures, he turned away sorrowing, seeking a new home in the far off wilds, where his feet had seldom if ever trod. He felt the white man was his greatest enemy; and as he explored the limits of his wild retreat he was pleased therewith. Then came those fearful forebodings that his posterity could not enjoy it after him; that his bones would lie there unmourned by the stranger who thoughtlessly treads among them.

---

* The Missionary.

The fear of the entire extinction of the race has from that time poisoned all our thoughts, for it hid itself away in the heart, like a worm in the choice bud; though enclosed in a little world of beauty and sweetness, yet eating away the very life thereof. Our children will change the religion of their forefathers; they will speak with the pale face as with brothers, and the pale face will listen to the words of those whom they have instructed in their own religion, and nourished with parental care. Will they not hear the words of their children? Yes, and plead for them with the white brothers, for they will love those for [Page 67] whom they have labored, and seek to do them good, and stay their hands from evil doing.

Now my brother thy heart is dark; a long, long night has come upon thee. It will struggle in vain for the full warmth of the bright hopes of youth, which warm and enliven the heart, as the sun does the earth at noonday, but it will no more shine upon thee in its usual brightness. It hath departed from thee no more to return, until thou shalt roam in the vast hunting-grounds of the Spirit-land, accompanied by the shades of thy fathers and friends. Now, my brother, listen to the counsel of a friend; let thine ears be open to all his words; they are for thy good.

Thou knowest that by the light of a well-known star, night-weary travellers, however sick at heart from grief or fatigue, may safely guide their footsteps homeward, for it cannot lie; for its feet never depart from the path which the Great Spirit has marked out for it to travel. It does not murmur at its hardships, nor yet tire of its daily journeyings. Though the path be long it is ever at its post.

Now let my brother's heart be comforted; let its strings take strength, that its grief may relax. Let it be open to receive the lesser light* of which I have spoken; that it may guide thy feet through the dark vale of old age, wherein is no light. When the heart is loaded down with sorrow, and when the bleak mountains of death shall appear in thy path, trust thyself still to its guidance. Though its light be feeble, yet it is constant and unvarying, as the Great Spirit from whom all light proceeds, whether high above our heads or beneath our feet. By its light, thou canst ascend that difficult mountain where the bright beams of the summer's sun, whose rays warmed thy youthful heart into greatness, shall burst full upon thy new sight, making thy heart which had grown cold through weariness, sing joyously with

---

* The Northern Star is prized by the Indians in the sun's absence.

warm delight. Let your ears be open to my words; let your heart feel their truth or falsehood, when I say thy child is not with the red people, but he will be a wanderer among many people, of many nations and colors; his foot shall leave its print in many lands, and he will feel himself a stranger among earth's children; his enemies shall be bitter and implacable, but his friends will be warm and true: trials such as few know, shall lurk in his path, yet he shall conquer, and return to his people with a firm step, an open hand, and a warm, true heart. He shall make them glad, and they shall rejoice together. My brother, what I said concerning him, when my hand rested on his infant head, I cannot find leave from [Page 68] the Spirit which dictates to my heart, to contradict now. Clouds have risen up, and with their dreariness obscured the brightness of our former hopes, and you doubt the probability, you almost say possibility of the truthfulness of my blessing upon the head of thy child. No! no! that were to suffer the evil Spirit to gain complete ascendancy over me at once; to darken my mind, to despoil me of my gift from the Great Spirit. I should but contradict myself; my tribe would lose all confidence in me, for I have ever contended that we had no need to worship the evil Spirit* ; that we should sin to offer sacrifice to him, to appease his anger; that in so doing, we only acknowledged his power as greater than the Great benevolent Spirit's, or at least as approaching to his authority. I have ever thought that if we could please the Great Spirit, he would preserve us from the power of all our enemies, for he at all times bestows good upon all his people, though their eyes are sometimes shut, and cannot discern the good from the evil which accompanies it. Yet it incurs his anger, and grieves the shades of our fathers in the spirit land, to see us bow in worship to the evil spirit, the mighty enemy of our race. I say again, the child shall be blessed by the Great benevolent Spirit, and shall yet do much good for his race, though trials shall rise up in his path, and with giant strength forbid his advance. The evil spirit shall seem to have overcome him times without number, and in various ways; yet he shall be sustained, and rise above the many snares which have been laid to accomplish his entire overthrow. He shall rise above, and triumph over all.

Come, my brother, let the light of hope shine again into thy heart, comforting and dispelling the clouds of darkness, which have gathered there!

---

* Some of the unchristian tribes worship and offer sacrifice to the Great Spirit, and offer some inferior sacrifice to appease the anger of the evil one.

Let the good Chief of a noble race take courage! His blood shall not yet cease to flow in the veins of his children; but their children's children shall pronounce thy name with reverence and gladness. Now take comfort, for thy people shall grow and flourish after a time, taking deep root in another land, and thy lost child shall return to make their hearts glad, and to rejoice in their midst, and they shall all make merry, for joy. Trust to the Good Spirit. Do not let thine ears be deaf to the voice of thy aged friend and counsellors. Mourn not as ye mourn for the dead, but rather ask the Great Spirit to protect and redeem the living; let thy former course hide thy grief from mortal eyes, and tell it only to him. Let us now return to the people. Let our [Page 69] tongues be silent when we meet them, lest the evil spirit ensnares us. Let our hearts hold silent counsel with the Great Spirit, and remember for ever our journey here, and our counselling together. We returned to the dwelling place of our people. I was worn with fatigue; my deep despair seemed to have exhausted itself in frequent outbursts of violent grief to which I had given way. A hopeless yet silent sorrow took possession of my mind. A constant pain was secreted there; hope would sometimes warm my heart it is true, contending strongly for its former undisputed sway, but when being forced to divide the spoil, would for a while, relinquish its endeavours to soothe me. I only realized its loss the more, and felt all the more solicitous for its return. Would to the Great Spirit that the Chief was present now, for here is his long lost and lamented son before us, exclaimed the old man.

I was impatiently, at times almost breathless listening to the words of the aged man. I did not dare to interrupt him, nor yet to ask even one of the many questions which arose in my mind, and trembled as it were on my tongue, but with the most intense anxiety, awaited the moment that his lips should cease to move. While he spoke, not a limb had been stirred, nor scarce a muscle moved, lest they should disturb the speaker, but when he ceased, all eyes which had been bent upon him, were turned upon me with an inquiring gaze which seemed to fasten me to my seat. I attempted to rise, but my limbs seemed to refuse to perform their office. I endeavored to speak, but my throat was swollen and painful in the extreme; my mouth was closed. The old man broke the silence by saying, here now is the blood of Choctaw, Cherokee, Creek, and Seminole. Let your ears be open to my words.

CERTAIN EVIDENCE THAT I AM THE SON OF THE CHOCTAW CHIEF.

I will tell you how I know he is my brother's son; will you hear, will your hearts understand, will your hands be open? They readily answered in the affirmative. He then proceeded, adding, he is not large and tall like his father, his mother very small, but his face very much like his father; so much I know him by his face. One day, many years ago, I visit Mosholeh Tubbee;* we like brothers; we love each other, so we go to Natchez, trade some, see the country and city; we [Page 70] take several with us, some women, Mosholeh Tubbee's wife and child, plenty of women and children go long; all camp on the bluff, where one tall house stands now to make light; then go down to city, walk all round much, trade some too, he very small child, he learn to run, squaw carry him, she tired, he very smart, he want to run; his father take him, put him down, see him run off so fast, laughs much, we on Powell's old pavement, all broke, he catch his foot, fall, cut his lip, hurt his toe on his right foot, almost break it, when well I saw the place on his toe; a lump grew on it, and a scar was left on his lip; his father laugh, say he know his child every where by these things.

Now I knew these scars were on me, yet had no knowledge of the cause of them. They all looked at them again and again. The old man stepped up and said, come my young Chief, shake hands with thy father's friend, and as he is no more, I will be a father to thee, and counsel you in all your ways. But you must be patient yet many days, but your time shall come. As thy years ripen, and thy knowledge becomes more extensive, seek to do good to thy people, and the Great Spirit shall do good to thee. He then asked how and where I lived. I related how and where I had spent most of my life. They could not bear to hear me relate in part many things which I have passed through, but begged me to tell them pleasanter parts of my story. They seemed pleased to learn that I had always loved the red people, and wished me to tell them when and where I first saw any of the tribes. After relating some facts which have been stated here, to which they listened with the deepest attention, I gave them an account of an interview I had with some Indians, who had encamped near Mr. James C. Williams' farm, which lay a few miles from Natchez; I made them a visit, which proved

---

* This man's father.

to be somewhat beneficial to me, and interesting to the Indians, and to Mr. Williams' family likewise. The same young Indian received me and called me his brother, and said that my father lost me while I was yet very small; that some had supposed that I had been stolen by some other tribe of Indians; others thought that the traders had taken me to the white settlement; and at other times they thought that wild animals had devoured me. He examined my feet, and looked at my lip. He seemed much pleased, and stated that he was going to travel about some, and then he would come back and take me to the Indian country. He regretted exceedingly that my father was not living to receive me. His name in English was Thomas. He did not return, and an Indian agent, known as Choctaw Smith, of Mississippi, told me he was dead.

[Page 71]"Well," said Puch-chee-Nubbee, "it is well I was the one to find and restore my brother's son. I feel that the time is near when I shall go in peace; and when I meet him, I will tell him all. Our spirits shall rejoice together over thee, in the spirit land."

The Indians then counselled together. Each one gave me something as a momento, calling me good young Chief. It was late, and the company returned home, but I remained with Puch-Chee-Nubbee. He introduced me to several young men, who proved very agreeable acquaintants; but Chief Powell was unfavorable to the plan of civilizing the Indians, and consequently thought that my influence among them would have a bad tendency. He feared that I would seek to do away the Indian's hatred for the whites, and establish friendship between them.

My stay among them had been short, yet full of interest to me. I promised Puch-chee-Nubbee and many others, to visit them at their homes in the West. I parted with them in peace, and returned to New Orleans, and prepared to leave for the Arkansas Territory. I was silent concerning what had passed in Florida. I really wished to speak of it to some of my friends, but my friend Puch-chee-Nubbee had charged me again and again, to say not a word until a future period, lest something should occur to deter me from my purpose.

VISIT TO THE CHOCTAW COUNTRY.

I was soon up the Arkansas river as far as Little Rock, where we stopped a short time. We also touched at the villages on the river, Fort Smith, and Fort Gibson. Here I found some Indians who accompanied me to their settlements. Here I met with my friends of Florida, who welcomed me to their homes. They were more comfortable, and better satisfied here than they had expected. All my Florida acquaintances wished to go with me to the Choctaw Nation. They said we would all go there together, as friends, and say nothing about my blood, and see if they could trace me out. They said I was young, and must let the aged talk for me.

The Choctaws received us kindly. When they asked who I was, they merely answered, "A friend." After a few days I was summoned to visit an old Interpreter, who had seen me pass by, and wished an interview. I went with my friends to his house. He said he had a reason for sending for me. He asked me to let him see my right foot [Page 72] naked. He then said that he was with my father when it was hurt. He looked at the scar on my lip. He then said that I reminded him so much of my father, that he had invited in some who had assisted him to search with my father for me. They mourned for my father, and rejoiced in my return. They told me where my father owned a very large tract of land, and they wished me to come and settle upon it. They called me Tubbee in disguise. I had always been very temperate, and the Temperance cause was beginning to have some spread among them. I formed an acquaintance with some who were engaged therein, and for a while lent my humble aid to the cause among the Indians.

At length it was agreed upon, and I was chosen to return to Mobile, and visit that portion of the Choctaws, who had refused to go West; but chose to remain upon their old hunting grounds, renting it from the citizens; or to hire out to them by the day, to obtain their sustenance. I had visited, hunted, &c., among them. I saw with pleasure that my efforts in the Temperance cause were truly appreciated among them. Oh! how it gladdened my heart to find the people of my departed father in such a thriving condition. Then came the sorrowful remembrance that my poor father drank fire-water. That was said to be his only fault, and I determined to spend time, strength, and property, to erase it. My friends furnished me a mule, and I visited, at the same time taking leave of friends. I visited some of the Mission Stations. I have always regretted that I did not go through the Southern portion of the tribe. They gave me permission to offer friends and home to any of the scattered families of the Indian tribes, who would come and live with them.

I departed with their best wishes for my success in my business with my pale-faced friends and my Indian brothers. I reached the crescent city in safety. I had heretofore visited Mobile, Pensacola, &c., and had been with the different companies on pleasure and fishing excursions along the coast; but my object was to try, at least, to do good. I visited the Indians in Alabama, as I had promised. I laid the facts of the case before them, and some of them said that they would go. Many promised that they would consider well, for my counsel was good. I have since learned that a goodly number moved over to the Arkansas Territory. And though they are somewhat behind the first settlers, bid fair to do well. It is also hoped that others will be induced to go. If I am prospered, I shall visit them again soon.

[Page 73] AN IMPORTANT IDEA SUGGESTED BY A DREAM—THE SAUCE PAN AND INDIAN TOMAHAWK CONVERTED INTO MUSICAL INSTRUMENTS.

I dreamed that I was an ancient Shepherd. One summer day, while my flock was resting in the shade, I sauntered out over the country. I came to a spot, where a pretty brook had once crept along, watering many flocks, But the brook was nearly gone, and the ground around was a miry swamp. There lay many sheep with broken and disjointed limbs, panting for life. They were not my sheep, and I was about to pass on. "What! said I, shall a shepherd pass a suffering flock, and offer no relief?" I returned, took them from the mire, and laid them on a carpet of red clover, under a shady tree. I was very thirsty, and as there was a little water in places, I began to contrive how to get a drink. I found that I had a saucepan in my pocket. With that I obtained a drink, and returned to my crippled sheep. I was very sorry for them, and wished to do something to relieve them. As I stood thus lamenting, I thought I heard a voice, saying: "Take the saucepan out of your pocket, and blow through the handle thereof, and there will come forth sweet strains of music, which shall cheer your flocks hereafter." I obeyed the command. The sheep and lambs raised their heads, listened attentively a few moments, then carefully arose to their feet. They slowly came towards me, bleating, as they nipped the clover from about my feet. The lambs were soon bounding away in playful gambols. I was delighted. I cast my eye over my left shoulder; and, to my astonishment, saw an exceedingly large flock of sheep which were mere skeletons; having no shepherd; they were obliged to live on white clover. I was very much concerned about them, and endeavored to devise some plan to induce them to follow me, and come over and feed on good pasture. In my concern and anxiety I awoke.

The interpretation was in my mind before I was conscious of being awake; as follows: The sheep were the Indians scattered, and driven by the pale-faces, until they were near unto famishing. I felt that if I could visit them with some simple instruments of music, that the harmony might melt the savage heart, and unite the broken and wasting tribes. The saucepan was ever before my mind after the dream.

I advised with some musicians and mechanics, who told me there could be no such instrument made; at least without one key. After some time, I again dreamed that I played upon it. I arose and marked it out on paper, and then went to the shop and made it after my pattern [Page 74] And this is the very saucepan with which I have enchanted both the red man of the forest, and the pale face of the city.

Reflecting still more upon this subject, for the dream had made an impression upon my soul, never to be worn off, I thought if the tomahawk, the Indian's most deadly weapon, could be made into an instrument of music, it would be coming nearer to the Indian's heart. So I set myself to work, and constructed one. With these two instruments, by the blessing of the Great Spirit, I felt I could harmonize broken and hostile tribes, and finally secure a union of all the members of the great Indian family, so that they might be refreshed and saved. But how could I do this? I was uneducated. I could neither read nor write.

CIRCUMSTANCES WHICH LED TO AN ACQUAINTANCE WITH MY WIFE, AND OUR MARRIAGE.

I was taught in a dream how I could be assisted in the difficulty. Many years ago, I dreamed of travelling up a large river, where I saw a female engaged in reading. Afterwards she knelt and prayed. I felt that the Lord had greatly blessed her, and although her face was from me, I saw in my dream that she would be my wife, and a helpmate indeed. So perfectly did I retain her image in my mind's eye, that I ever thought I should know her if I could see her. I had an idea that this river was the Ohio. Therefore when I could make it convenient, and felt myself competent to support a wife, I started up the Ohio. In travelling, I was sure this was the same river, for every thing looked as natural as if I had seen it before. When at Cleveland and Sandusky, I was disappointed in not finding her. Here I saw her travelling in another direction. I then returned to New Orleans, where I saw her moving towards me. This I considered a good omen. I then left and went up the Mississippi. I there saw her look earnestly at me, and smile. When at Gelana I saw her again. I was going from her. She looked sorrowful, and beckoned me to return. I stopped and returned by the first boat, and went on shore at the village where the boat stopped.

At the mouth of the Iowa, I met some Indians, who had come down in their boats from Iowa city. I played them a tune, they were much pleased, and invited me to go to their camps. I went with them, for I had already given myself up to circumstances. The next morning I went up to Iowa city. I saw and knew the house in which my wife was, and begged an invitation to call. I will now let my wife speak for herself, [Page 75] for she does not like to hear me say that we made an engagement the first day, made an acquaintance the next, and was married so soon.

I was born Dec. 28, 1817, in Western New York. My father was a Mohawk Chief, a most excellent man; a great friend to civilization, and never took fire-water. But alas! he did not believe the Bible. My mother was related to the Delewares; she believed the Bible, though she made no profession of christianity.

From my earliest recollection I was the subject of religious impressions, made on my mind from a dream which I had when about two years old. I do not know that I had any knowledge of God previous to this.

The dream was as follows: I thought that a person possessing a most lovely countenance, came to me and said: "Little child, do you know you have a Father in Heaven?" I answered, "How can I have two fathers?" He said my Father in Heaven had only lent me to this father; that I was given to a fallen people to do them good. He said that my Father in Heaven still loved me very much; and had sent him to bless me. He told me that he spoke of the God of Heaven, who made me, and all things, and explained something of his attributes. He told me I must learn to read the Bible, where I should find his will, and what I must do to be saved. He then put his hand on my head, blessed me, and taught me to pray. He told me if I would continue to do this, which I promised to do, that my Heavenly Father would give me whatever I wanted. He then told me that if I was faithful, I should go and dwell with him in a never-ending eternity. I could not at first understand what these things could mean. I refused to play, and spent all my time in conversing upon them. My pleadings with my father to go to school were such, that he permitted me to go, carrying me in his arms every day, I made rapid progress in learning, and before I was eight years old, I had read the Bible through by course. During this time my father permitted christian people to come to our house and instruct me in the things of religion. And when in the course of this instruction, I learned that the Saviour died for all, and especially for me, my heart was overwhelmed with gratitude and love. Before I was ten years old, I was allowed the privilege of being baptised in his dear name. O, to put on Christ in this precious ordinance was sweet to my thirsty soul. And now I appeal to the experienced christian to supply what I am unable to say further. Before this my father had removed to the Western Reserve, and settled temporarily. Some of my people went [Page 76] to Green Bay, where they now reside. I went to school near Cleveland, Ohio. Afterwards my father removed to Missouri, and settled on the south side of the river, near Fort Leavenworth. Several years afterwards he made a visit into the Iowa, taking his family with him.

One morning while here, casting an eye into the street, I saw an Indian whom I knew must be a stranger. Although I had no thought of ever seeing him again, yet I called my sisters, saying, "do you see that Indian brave? I never saw or heard of him before, but I *shall* know him well, for he will be my husband." This was about my first attempt as a joke.

He afterwards met my sister in the street, and said to her, "do you live in that white cottage? "Yes sir," was the reply. "Well," said he, "there is a person at your house who wishes to see me, and when you return, you may tell her I would like to call on her to day." She promised to do so, and when she came home and related what had happened, we hardly knew what to think of it.

Late in the afternoon he called. He spoke familiarly with the sister he had met, and asked her to introduce him. My mother, two sisters, and the lady of the house were present. When he came to me, he looked earnestly in my face, and said, "Yes, you are the one." My mother soon stepped forward and said, "Come tell us which of my daughters wished to see you?" He came towards me and said, "this is the one. Come here and I will convince you that I have seen her before, by showing you a certain mark on her face." He then said to me, "will you marry me?" "O yes," I replied. He drew my arm through his, and bowing to the company, asked if we should not make a good match? My father then came in, and he and all the rest laughed at the joke. We all drank tea together. After tea he offered to play us a tune. This did not please me, for I feared he might be a dissipated, irreligious character, like many other travelling musicians. The first instrument he used was the flute. He then took up his sauce-panana and said, "will the company accept of a tune from this?" All were very solicitous except myself. He then related the dream which had led to its construction. My feelings were changed. I was now willing to become his shepherdess in a cause which had engrossed the most of my attention through life, and was still dearer to me than all things else. When he bade me good night he said, "can I depend on your word?" I replied, "I always keep my word."

When I was alone I pondered over what had passed. I supposed it [Page 77] all a joke and yet I half wished he was speaking from his heart. The next morning he returned. We were all seated in the parlor with some visitors. We talked of his plan and endeavoured to devise the best means of carrying it into effect. I said nothing of my own early convictions in regard to my people or any other matter in relation to myself. He told me that he could neither read nor write, and added, I am a naturalist, I must teach them on natural principles to begin with. The Lord has provided me a help meet in you, to teach them the truths of religion, by precept and example. We can be of use to each other, and by uniting our destines, do a good work for our poor people. I could not speak. He proceeded by mentioning my childhood and experience in religion. I at length interrupted him by asking who told you this? He said he had these thoughts respecting me when he first saw me in his dream; that he only mentioned them to see if they were true. He then told me that he was not jesting at all, the night before, that he was as well acquainted with me as though he had known me for years.

The Bible says: "it is not good for man to be alone," and I have come to receive an answer to my first proposal. My time is short; tell me truly, will you marry me and my cause. I will pass by the thousand misgivings of my heart. Worldly matters had not been named between us; he had not told me, only by his manner, that he was more pleased with me than others. My answer was, I am not prepared to give other answer than I gave last night. He then seemed very much delighted and said he was happy to find me and hear me answer in his favor. He then told me of his travels in search of me. In a short time I gave him my word not to be recalled, that I would be his wife. He then told me he must be married the next day. To this I could not agree, No! no! I was willing to marry him in a few months, or weeks, at least, if he would set the time and come to my father's in Missouri. He said we must not look so far ahead, but to do all we found to do, as fast as we could, for our work was great. I felt the truth of these remarks, and was willing to practice them in all other points. We retired to a room alone, where I begged and pleaded with him to split the difference at least. But he was not to be moved from his purpose. He did not say that he would never come, but said that we must be married the next day or bid me farewell for a long time, perhaps forever. I gave him my hand to say adieu; my heart failed me. I asked myself if it could thus set aside an opportunity of realizing its long cherished [Page 78] hopes, if it could thus allow perhaps a false modesty to step between it and duty. I greatly admired firmness in man. I knew my parents did not fully understand his plan, although it seemed so beautiful to me. Well, said I, ask my parents, if they can, I will consent. They did consent, providing he would not take me South, and we were married. I remained with my parents. After a short time he returned to the South. We have been blessed with a son, a fine healthy child, possessing a strong mind. Also two daughters. I have watched over my heart with a careful eye, lest I should place them between me and my duty, and the Father should take them to himself. After we had been married sometime, I heard my husband speak of Mr. Job Daone. He stated that he stopped at his hotel near Cleveland, Ohio, when he first set out to find his wife. I had been in his hotel several times, and found upon inquiry, that if he had come within a year or so of his first dream he would have come where I was at school, before we removed West. Although my little ones still needed a mother's care, we now and then made short visits among the tribes, which was very pleasant indeed. In 1842 my husband visited Kentucky for the purpose of seeing the young men of the Choctaws who were at White Sulphur Academy, more commonly known as Dick Johnson's Indian School. He played for several encampments, &c. He was in the South most of 1844. As he was returning home he formed some acquaintances in St. Louis. And in 1845, gave an entertainment at Planter's House and several places of amusement in that city, where he has many warm friends.

He visited many towns that winter in Missouri and Illinois, endeavoring to make friends with those winning sounds so peculiar to himself, and then interest them for the Indian family. He returned to his family, and in 1846, by his earnest solicitation, I left my little charge with my parents, while I visited with my husband the principal towns in Missouri, Kentucky, Indiana, and Ohio, among which were Cincinnati and Madison. We then returned to our family. We remained at home a short time, and then began a tour among the Indians. Afterwards we visited the Iowa tribes, then returned to Missouri. Travelled up the Missouri river by land, visiting those uncivilized tribes far above the Council Bluffs. After much labor and anxiety on our part, our fondest hopes were realized. I rejoiced that I had lived to see the grey-haired chiefs of the forest sit in tears at my husband's feet, while he discoursed with their hearts through his simple instruments. Their astonishment exceeded anything I ever saw. He could make them understand that the Great [Page 79] Spirit had given him this gift, that he might counsel with, and make friends of all the tribes. When their hearts were softened down with melody we could introduce the gospel with good effect. In the course of a few days, my husband could get enough of their tongue to make them, with the help of signs and gestures, understand what I read. They would soon ask, your tribe, what is it? On being told Choctaw, they would mourn, and say, Great Spirit bless Choctaw much, he no bless us; come you say, let our tribe be your tribe. You be our chief and counsellor. They manifested great signs of sorrow when we told them we must return, and would not consent until we had promised them another visit. Afterwards we visited the tribes along the frontiers. There they were equally astonished, perhaps not so much overwhelmed as those in their wild state. We spent June and July, and a part of the month of August, visiting along the frontiers. September 1, 1847, we came down the Missouri river, on our way to Washington City, D. C. My husband gave several concerts, in cities and towns. We constantly endeavoured to interest the citizens in behalf of the Indians. Pleading with them that the present home of the civilized tribes should be a permanent location. We were well received at Washington city; not only by the President and Lady, but by the citizens also. We

visited Virginia, then returned to Washington, from thence through Maryland and Delaware, then to Philadelphia. We also took a tour through all
the cities in Pennsylvania. Afterwards returning, visited several places, and
proceeded to New York, where we arrived May 20, 1848.

August 28, we left our kind friends in New York, and ere long reached
New Haven, Ct. In order that my friends may form an idea of the pleasure
and gratification I receive in travelling, I will make a short extract from
my journal written while in New Haven, dated Tontine House, Tuesday
29, 1848; and as I wrote this little work by half-days and half-hours as best
I could while travelling, let me quote, writing every spare moment, which
made me enjoy the more a pleasant walk through the public square, so
nicely fenced in with dear old elm trees, tall and beautiful indeed. They
surely recall pleasing associations of home to the mind of the stranger.
Strolled through the ground surrounding Yale College, which far surpassed
in beauty and size my anticipations. We then crossed over to the cemetery
near by It is enclosed by an iron railing; a large structure of Egyptian sculp-
ture forming the gate-way. It was too late to walk through the grounds; yet
I could not resist a strong desire to step within its limits, for it is [Page 80]
good for me to stand where the dead rest, and oh! shall I, who so much love
to ramble where they sleep, shall I fear to lie down and rest with them when
my measure is full? God forbid.

August 31st.—Rode out again. Oh! what a lovely spot! I can but conclude
that some hundreds of beautiful country seats, or I might say American
palaces, had agreed to take up their walks, parks, gardens, summer-houses
and pleasure grounds, and called together here to luxuriate in the sea
breeze, and withal to hold council under the old elms, which look to me
like so many guardian angels stretching forth their giant arms in their defence. Again they once sheltered the councillors of the red men who assembled here in olden time—they must have loved them. Oh! children of
the forest where hast thou fled.

March, 1849, found us in New Bedford, Mass., having visited some of
the principal cities in the New England Sates. Circumstances rendered me
very anxious for a speedy return to the West. We returned by the way of
New York city, from thence to Philadelphia, then to Harrisburg, where we
took the canal to Pittsburgh, Pa. The canal packets were so crowded with
California Emigrants that we were forced to leave our baggage behind us.
This was quite unexpected to us. We had no time to unpack, consequently
whatever was valuable was left in its place. We stopped at several cities by

the way, and expected that the freight-boat would get through first. We waited in Pittsburg a few days—it came not. We expected to make a short stay in St. Louis, and business men, even the forwarding merchants, advised us to go on, and our goods would overtake us there. I was scarcely able to travel, and we proceeded immediately to St. Louis. We landed the first day of May. The cholera was at work in every street. It came nearer; but my spirits and hopes increased according to the danger, and I suffered no more from alarm when death occured next room to mine, than when I heard it was only a few doors off. Our trunks and boxes came at length, but some person or persons had taken from them all that was valuable; the locks on two of them had been broken, and one of them had the hinges taken off. Next came the great fire, and a part of what was left by the theives was destroyed by the pitiless element. This great fire occured about 24 hours before our youngest child, Mosholeh Tubbee first saw light, which occured May 21, 1849, at St. Louis, Mo. About the first of July we gathered up what thieves, fire, and expenses had not swallowed up, and started up the Missouri river. We had left a small well furnished farm in Lafayette county, [Page 81] Mo., When we returned, we found that through false debts and sham sales, everything had passed into the hands of others. We remained in Lexington, Lafayette county, Mo., two weeks, counselled with Mr. Sharp, attorney at law, entered suit for the recovery of our property, &c. The cholera was raging there at that time; we were weary of the sorrow and suffering that necessarily followed in its track, and concluded to visit the Indian tribes along the Missouri river, with many of whom we were acquainted. But alas! as in other days, the (pale-face) California Emigrants had left the scourge behind them, and many of our friends had fallen a prey to its ravages. When it first appeared they were alarmed at its violence, and for a few days was very fatal, but stronger potions of medicine were prepared, and relief found therein.

It is generally supposed by many novel readers, that the Mohican tribe of Indians has become extinct; this, however, is not exactly the case. Although, as their name denotes, the more western tribes once looked upon them as a great and powerful people, who possessed the beautiful regions from whence the sun rose, diffusing warmth and blessings innumerable upon all their lands. There are a few hundred of them still living. A portion of them would never remove from Norwich, Ct. Another portion of them are in Green Bay. This portion of them undertook a few years back to emigrate to Missouri territory. A number of families, Hendricks the Chief, consisting of a large family of sons, Kunkapots, Dockstatter, &c., went out first. Their journeying had wearied them, and the fevers that those living in that climate are subject to, soon carried off many, even whole families. Under these circumstances letters were written home and the others refused to come, but wished to go farther north, mentioning Fort Snelling, Iowa. The government could point out no particular spot of land for them, and they settled on a portion of the land held by the Delawares. Oh! if there is a lovely fairy-like land on earth, just fresh from under Dame Nature's hand, it surely is this. My powers of description would fail me should I attempt to portray its loveliness. The Mohican or Stockbridge (a name given by the English) village, is situated five or six miles from Fort Leavenworth, fifteen miles above the Kansas river. The main road leading from Independence, Mo., to the fort, passes through the settlement of the Delawares, leaving the Wyandotts to the right, at the mouth of the Kansas. A remnant of the Muncies are thereabouts also. As it winds its way towards the fort, it passes through one of the most beautiful praries it was ever my lot to behold. It leaves the main part [Page 82] of the small village of Stockbridge a half mile to the right, half buried as it were in the timber on the Missouri river bluff, which here skirts the prairie. Three years before we left them all church members, now we found them all dissipated save one, Eli Hendricks. A fearful misunderstanding had arisen through viein g how there could be so many different yet right ways to worship one God, all taken from the Bible.

As I am obliged to be brief, let me add, that it caused the missionary to be abused and removed, consequently they had no church nor school. We were informed of the sad change for the worse, before we reached there—how they made a ball every Saturday night for the soldiers, Californians, and discharged soldiers, who herded cattle for the fort; that they all lay drunk over Sunday. &c. &c.; and that we could not reclaim them. We had the little good we hoped to do in our eye, and we trusted to the Great Spirit for the result. But our cup was not yet full of disappointment. All our best intentions and bright anticipations were suddenly blasted, just as we thought them about to be realized. We had taken much pains to furnish a house well, filled it to overflowing, that they might see the comforts of an industrious, sober life. Many became convinced, and promised to reform. We laid in our winter stores, and went after our older children who had been left with their grand parents. The officers at the fort had been extremely kind to my husband. They had offered him any assistance he might need in tracing out those who were smuggling in liquor, thereby enriching themselves by basely degrading their fellow men. He had been invited to the (Sabbath morning) drunken revel, but had not accepted. There were many threats that were to be put in force if he broke up the trade, many stories in circulation tending to turn the minds of the Indians against him; but his motives were good, and we saw no evil. On our return we learned that all had been burned. I leave the reader to judge whether it was better or worse; all was gone; sold out in the settlements here and there. It was done over the line, there was no redress.

We went to Weston. Mo., and spent the winter as best we could, having nothing to do to any advantage. In the course of the winter, the Doctor and our oldest son, Solon, went to St. Louis to see the principal agent of Indian affairs but he was gone. In the Spring, he thought that he should enjoy himself better in another part, farther from where our misfortune occurred; for we often met with what perhaps had been a present to us and now owned by another. We removed to Independence, [Page 83] Mo., The Doctor had been practicing medicine, whether travelling or not, and now we had depended upon it for a support.

There is a prejudice existing against the Indian in the minds of many along the frontier. If he is civilized, they laugh at his attempts to imitate the pale-face. I had lived at Independence scarce six weeks, when a noted gambler came to my door, one o'clock Sabbath morning, and called me out of bed that he might insult me. He was formerly of Natchez, Miss. He had undertaken it the day before, but was prevented. The citizens, most of them, treated me with respect, but ever after this, when this man could see me he would try to quarrel with me. He said he had always known me; that I was no physician, &c. &c. Some persons who seemed near death called on me, under this prejudice, and by the help of God they recovered and are living. My enemies had accused Mrs. Tubbee of forging the certificates from the east; but when those were published from the persons I had relieved there in that city, he only threatened the more. I bore this one year, striving to do the best I could. He was rich—a liberal, genteel, drunken gambler. He had put many of these threats into execution, but he had plenty of money to pay his fine—was ready and willing, be it ever so large, and a bottle of the best to treat all the authorities. He made them and their wives and daughters most costly presents when he wished to get drunk and do his devilment. I had the promise of protection from the civil law, if I looked there for protection. My practice as a physician was rapidly improving, but

I could not brook his abuse, and I sold (or rather gave) out what we had by industry collected again. I felt that I had rather seek friends elsewhere, and have since been travelling in the Western States and Canada I sell medicines for cases, sell recipes, and hold musical entertainments, &c.

I am no poetess, yet a strange sensation come over me on one occasion, on parting with my husband as follows: he was in readiness to go away, and went to the landing to see about a boat. There was one there ready to go out, and he went aboard and was soon under way. I was awaiting his return; I heard the boat, I felt that he was gone I sat me down, (for I could not stand,) tears fell like rain as I sung the following lines, as fast as though I had always known them. They seem to me not wholly without merit, yet they must be imperfect, for there has [Page 84] never been a word changed. I am only induced to insert them by the urgent request of my husband.

> Then fare thee well, my lover,
> I cannot bid thee stay,
> For that thou must watch over
> Calls thee from me away;
> And I must be contented
> To part from thee awhile,
> Although my heart relenteth,
> And tears my eyes do fill.
>
> Oh! could I have but seen thee,
> And pressed thy lips with mine,
> And heard thee say, God bless thee,
> In that fond way of thine;
> Oh! I could have borne thy absence,
> Without so much regret,
> Having the sweet assurance,
> That thou dost love me yet.
>
> I know, on thy returning,
> Thou wilt this lone one greet;
> My heart's already burning,
> I long my love to meet.
> Although we're forced awhile to part,
> We'll ever constant prove—

Each aspiration of the heart
Shall be in perfect love.

Oh! that the winds could bear me
Thy breath while thou art gone,
To comfort and to cheer me
While I am thus alone
Should misfortunes e'er o'ertake thee,
Oh! then remember me;
Should other friends forsake thee,
Thine own I still shall be.

LAAHCEIL OKAH TUBBEE.REFERENCES, &c.

Being about to insert a word from one or two of my Louisiana friends, their images and kindness come up before me, overwhelming my heart with gratitude. Though years have passed and I am far away, yet my mind is busy tracing the outlines of the dear square, where we assembled for the Governor's review. Near the centre stood Gov. Mouton, and Aid, the very animal on which he rode, looking about him, prouder [Page 85] than his fellows, as if conscious that he bore about one of the honorable men of the earth. Honorable for the high title which his countrymen had conferred upon him, but more so because of the many acts of kindness, his philanthrophic heart had prompted him to perform.

The stars and stripes unfurled above their heads, waving gracefully to and fro in the gentle breeze, as if thus endeavoring to acknowledge the pleasure of gracing such an occasion; the gallant officers at their posts; warm hearted privates standing in unbroken ranks, yet forming no stronger line than the friendship of their brave and manly hearts; and then the worthy citizens of standing, a little way off, smilingly tipping the beaver in welcome recognition of their friends; and when the signal was given for taking up the line of march, then came the thrilling notes of the fife, brought forth with three fingers of one hand, while I ingeniously managed to wave my cap to both officers and privates, gentlemen and ladies, while making my humble obeisance to all. And as the sound of martial music fell on the soldiers' ear, new vigor and elasticity seemed to be added to their measured step. Each face is still familiar in the mind's eye, though many of them have felt the scorching heat of a Mexican sun; and some of them suffered exceedingly, unused to the hardships of a soldier's life; then some have sickened and died in that far off land, without the soothing and necessary care of watchful and loving wives, anxious mothers, or tender sisters.

O, could I have played that funeral dirge, and dropped a tear on the grave of a friend, right willingly would I have performed that task. I could then have returned to private life. Peace to the ashes of the noble dead, who await in a stranger's land the sounding of the archangel trump. May the kind heartedness of the young maiden of Mexico prompt her to scatter the seeds of those beautiful flowers congenial to her own sunny clime, over his lonely grave, there to bud and bloom, diffusing their fragrance over the unmarked spot, an appropriate substitute for the sighs and tears of their friends at home. True he might not have been her friend in life, but it is pleasure to serve in sickness and death, one who was not a friend.

The bare mention of the name of Capt. Charles F. Hosea, serves to call up the multiplicity of favors conferred upon me. How often has he called me his son. And well he might, for he acted a father's part towards me, and I really loved him with all the tenderness a fond child could feel for a kind and indulgent parent.

Then again I bring to mind the American Theatre, where many have [Page 86] endeavoured to forget the cares and realities of life in gazing upon the enchanting performances of the stage. There they, admiring the scenes, have watched with intense emotion the rise and fall of the curtain before some of the most illustrious actors of which the new or old world can boast. But now the scenes were changed in reality, and the theatre was converted into a drill room for the Washington battalion and instead of theatrical songs of music of the orchestra, the roll of the drum and shrill notes of the fife now and then caused the old walls to echo with "Hail Columbia happy land; then comes "Yankee Doodle," unawares upon the attentive ear, like the sight of rich dessert, when one has already dipped deep into a plentiful dinner, yet must surely taste of all the fine flavor of the last, causing it to be as acceptable as the first, when the appetite was keen. Dear old Louisiana, how I love to recall those scenes! I loved them then—I love them still! Yes, I have good reason to love thee ever. You gave me protection—a happy home. In the day of sorrow your kind-hearted sons and daughters were my friends. Your memory shall be treasured up.

From R. B. Mitchell, Sub-Agent of Indian Affairs, in reply to a letter of

Introduction from Mr. S. B. Fithian, of Columbia, Mo.

COUNCIL BLUFFS, June 10, 1847.

SIR:—Your favor of the 18th January, 1847, came safely to hand, and Mr. Okah Chubbee (or Tubbee) is hereby granted permission to visit all the Indian tribes under my control, and I will render his visit as comfortable as possible.

Yours, respectfully,

R. B. MITCHELL, Ind. Sub-Ag't.

TO OKAH TUBBEE, (formerly known as WM. McCAREY.)
SIR:—In compliance with your request to give my testimony of your standing as a citizen and musician in Louisiana, I can hardly hope to add anything, to the respect which must be given to the recommendation of you, by Col. Dakin, whose high standing and extensive acquaintance must render his letter to the President of the United States, of much more service to you, than anything which could come from me. But I do not hesitate to add my testimony to his, of my knowledge of your good standing in New Orleans, and of the general admiration of your talents, as a musician, unequalled perhaps by any flutist in the world. And from my knowledge of some of the facts related by you in your account of your life, I have no reason to doubt your whole account of your parentage, &c.

[Page 87]You have my best wishes that you may meet with the success which your remarkable talents as a musician deserve.

Respectfully,

P. B. TYLER.

Springfield, Mass. Oct. 9th, 1818.

From Mr. Medill, Commissioner of Indian Affairs.

An individual identified as William McCarey, who has ascertained from the Indians, that he is by birth a Choctaw Indian, alledges, which I have no reason to doubt, for he has come highly recommended by James H. Dakin, Col. Reg. Louisiana Volunteers, to the President of the United States, as a man whose character, both as a musician and a citizen, has been unexceptionable, in Louisiana. That for many years he resided among the whites, thereby losing the means of tracing his parentage, until assisted by the Indians of the Six Nations, and others, who had been friends and acquaintances of his father. He has complied with their wishes, by taking the name of Chubbee or Tubbee, which they know to be the name of his father, which name is found to be affixed to treaties made with the Choctaw Indians.

W. MEDILL, Commissioner.

Office of Indian Affairs,

Washington, Nov. 27, 1848.

THE STATE OF MISSOURI.

To all persons to whom these presents shall come:—Greeting.

Know ye that Okah Tubbee having on the 23rd day of December, A. D. 1850, paid to George W. Buchanan, Collector within and for the County of Jackson, the sum of two dollars and fifty cents, being the annual tax imposed on him as a practicing Physician. These are therefore to License and authorize the said Okah Tubbee to practice Medicine within the State of Missouri for twelve months from this date.

In testimony whereof, I, John R. Sweanger, Clerk of the County Court within and for the County aforesaid, have hereto set my hand and affixed the seal of said Court, at Office, in the City of Independence, this 23rd day of December, A. D. 1850.

JOHN R. SWEANGER, Clerk.

Granted this 23rd day of December, 1850.

GEO. W. BUCHANAN, Collector.

Mr. Tubbee:

Princeton, In. May 8th, 1851.

DEAR SIR:—When you was in Princeton a few days since, I attended your lectures on *"natural principles"* which was truly amusing and pleasing, you are truly a great naturalist, and I can safely recommend you to the public patronage. The history of your life, written by your wife is truly amusing. You are at liberty to have this published in any respectable newspaper. You have the Printer's thanks for the tickets to your GRAND CONCERT.

Yours, truly,

T. K. DAVIDSON.

[Page 88] Terre Heevti, Indiana, June 1, 1851.

Rev. Alfred Wright:

DEAR SIR:—This will be handed you by Dr. Okah Tubbee of the Choctaw Nation, who has been spending a few days at the Phoenix House in this place, he has given a Musical Concert while here to a large audience, all of whom appeared much gratified with his performance, and it affords me much pleasure to bear witness to his uniform gentlemanly deportment while amongst us,

Very truly your friend,

C. MAIR.

Green Castle, 10th June, 1851.

Having been favored with a partial acquaintance with the bearer hereof, Dr. Okah Tubbee of the Choctaw Nation, during his short stay in this place, and being much pleased with his intelligence and gentlemanly bearing and deportment, I take much pleasure in introducing him to the acquaintance and favorable attention of all worthy citizens.

Our acquaintance rather accidental, but facilitated by his having knowledge of the relations of my son-in-law, who is partially connected with the same tribe.

The Public may be well assured that the Doctor will not abuse any confidence which may be placed in him in regard to any performance he may propose.

REV. THOMAS MORROW.

Dayton, July 7, 1851.

BRO. LAUNDER:—Permit me to introduce to your acquaintance, my friend, Dr. Okah Tubbee, who has been in our city for some two weeks, and has proved himself to be a mason, a gentleman, and a skilful Physician. He has received the greatest attention from the craft in this place, and we now recommend him to your favorable notice.

Thomas Launder, Esq.

Yours fraternally.

JOS. W. CLAYTON.

To whom it may concern.

This may certify that the bearer. Doctor Okah Tubbee, has been stopping at my house for the last two days, and gave two of his Musical Entertainments to a delighted audience. I would also state that he conducts himself with propriety, and is a gentleman in every respect.

Batana, Aug. 9, 1851.

B. G. TRIDALE.

Pelham, C. W. 27th Sep. 1851.

To all whom it may concern.

We hereby certify that we have heard Dr. Okah Tubbee (the Choctaw Chief) perform on the Flute and other Instruments, and as a *natural* performer on those Instruments, he is in our opinion unrivalled, and we hereby recommend him to the kind consideration of all lovers of music.

JOHN FRASER, M. D.
J. R. LAVELLS.
JOHN S. PRICE.

[Page 89]As a natural Flautist, Dr. Okah Tubbee is the finest I have ever heard, *J. McCARROLL, H. M. Custom House Officer, Niagara Falls, C. W.*

St. John's, C. W. 4th Oct. 1851.

Having been present at a Musical Entertainment given by Dr. Okah Tubbee in this place. I take pleasure in saying that I was delighted beyond the power of language to express with his truly wonderful performance. I would advise all who have a particle of "music in their souls," to embrace the first opportunity to hear this wonderful man. He is not a musician, he is music personified.

ZENAS FELL.

This is to certify that Dr. Okah Tubbee has performed in this place, in the Odd Fellows' Hall, and his extraordinary performance on the Flute, excited "general admiration." The Doctor also gave a very interesting Lecture on the habits of the Choctaw Nation.

J. AMSDEN,
JOHN ADAMS,
THOMAS CARLISLE,
L. J. WEATHERLY.

Dunville, C. W. Oct. 11, 1851.

Colpoy's Bay, Indian Settlement, 23rd March, 1852.

MY DEAR SIR: I have the honor to inform you that having received one of your circulars, which was sent to me by one of the Ladies in Toronto, which I am sorry to say in reply to the above:—my dear brother, you know that I was bound for my duty on that occasion, so when the time came on for home, the stage will not wait on me to stop a few minutes for to come and see my dear brother and my dear sister. I was very sorry indeed in forgetting you, but if I live next year, I shall be independent like you, and can manage my own business in all quarters of our land. I hope my dear brother, you will forgive your dear brother, of being absent from your representation in the Hall.

I hope you have good luck and prosperity of your business in the city, and find good friends yet.

I am at liberty to request you what circumstance and situation would you be required, if these three tribes of the Chippeways will employ you for a Physician among them, what will be the salary per year. I have told them about you, they are anxious to get you one of them, you will be pleased to write to me immediately about this request.

The direction will be J. H. Beaty, Interpreter, Colpoy's Bay, Owen Sound Post Office. Please to give my best compliments to sister Okah Tubbee.

I am your affectionate friend.

PAH-DAH-SONG,
J. H. BEATTY.

STATE OF MISSOURI.

To all who shall see these presents:—Know ye that Okah Tubbee, having on the 22nd day of December, 1849, paid to M. N. Owen, Collector within and for the county of Platte, the sum of two dollars and fifty cents, being the annual tax imposed on him as a Physician; therefore [Page 90] the said Okah Tubbee is hereby authorized to practice as such, at any one place within said State for twelve months, ending the 22nd day of December, 1850.

In testimony whereof, I, Daniel P. Lewis, Clerk of the County Court of the county of Platte have affixed the seal of said Court, this 22nd day of December, 1849.

Granted this 22nd day of December, 1849.

DANIEL P. LEWIS, Clerk.
M. N. OWEN, Collector.

MY DEAR SIR:—A worthy brother and personal friend of mine, request me to ask the question, and wishes you to send me the necessary receipt to cure a "weakness of the kidneys," whereby he cannot retain his water, particularly when he gets his feet the least damp. This weakness was brought on after maturity, by some complaint, or the Medicines for the same. Now will you prescribe for this case as soon as you can, and send me word. I cut out two copies of your Certificates and will send you more, or the originals if you wish them.

I have the originals of the Certificates of which I now send you the "printed copy," having published them such way in my paper.

New York, January 18, 1850.

R. R. BOYD.

Weston, Township of York, March 3rd, 1852.

Doctor Okah Tubbee has given two Concerts at this village. His astonishing execution on a common Flute, and indeed on several other instruments have delighted us beyond measure. His musical taste is exquisite, and we, with much pleasure, recommend him in his travels, to all lovers of the Art as every way worthy of a liberal patronage.

JOHN A. DONALDSON,
J. STOUGHTON DENNIS,
E. S. NIBBILET, Weston Hotel.

Weston, 3rd March, 1852.

Dear Romain:—Allow me to introduce to your notice one of our Indian Chiefs, Okah Tubbee, he goes to your village to hold a Concert there; we have had two nights of him here, and to say the least of him, he is one of the best Flute Players I have ever heard, and I know you will be delighted with him. Altogether he is a fine fellow that I know you will like very much. He also has with him Mrs. Tubbee, a most interesting intelligent person, and a fine specimen of the Indian tribe. He has our best wishes from Weston, and wishing him every success we leave him in your hands.

Yours truly.

DONALDSON.

My dear Donaldson:—I am in receipt of yours, and in reply would say that I am much pleased with the introduction of the parties herein mentioned. I shall exert myself to the utmost to make them comfortable, and to secure them a full house. I regret much, that your note came to hand at such a late hour, for I feel deeply interested with the parties.

Yours truly,

P. Z. ROMAIN.

Cooksville, March 3, 1852.

[Page 91]June 10th, 1851.

Mosholch Tubbee, the principal Chief of the Choctaw Nation, was killed by accident in the city of Maysville, Mason county, Kentucky, about the year 1826 or 1827, while on his way to Washington City, on some business of his nation.

He had put up in the city of Maysville for the night, at a hotel upon Water Street. The bank of the river opposite to the public house was very steep, near twenty-five feet high, and walled up with stone. After night, the old Chief stepped out of the house, crossed the street, and walked over the bank,—it being very dark. He was taken up in a few minutes afterwards, but so badly was he bruised by the fall, that he did not live more than twenty-four hours. His burial which I attended, took place the day after his death, in the city.

The above facts are substantially true.

JOHN COWGILL.

Call upon any of the old citizens of the city of Maysville, Ky., and they will, no doubt, be able to give more particulars, and also show you his grave,

Attest,

WASHINGTON WALLS.

REAL INDIAN MEDICINES.

It has long been the study of the Medical Faculty to check the progress of disease in the human system. They have often failed, however, owing to the practice of impregnating the body with Mineral Medicines, thereby confirming instead of removing the disease.

When Couut La Selle expressed his astonishment that there were no cripples or deformities among the Indian tribes, from the east to the west, one of the Chiefs replied,—"You have men to mend limbs, that were taught by men to do so; we obtain our knowledge from the Great Spirit. Perfect knowledge comes from the clouds; yours comes from man only." A celebrated Missionary, John Zimmuman, was told, in answer to like questions,—"Our God forms not his mortals without intelligence; he wisely ordained that we should all possess the capacity of supplying our wants, healing our wounds, and restoring our fractured bones." I need not quote their late sayings to show that these children of nature, fully rely upon the life preserving qualities of the flowers and plants that beautify their "Mother Earth," for aid to supply the wants of each invalid. This knowledge is handed down from one to another. Although Okah Tubbee's early years were spent with the whites, yet it has been his care and delight, to learn from his people, the art of healing with those harmless medicines. He has practiced more or less, for many years, and has succeeded in curing cases that had i thstood for years the efforts of the best practitioners. From his success in curing diseases of long standing, he feels it a duty and a privilege to communicate with those who labor under afflictions of all kinds. Rheuma ic Affections, Spinal and Nervous Affections, Toothache, Scrofula, Piles, Cancer, Tetter, Sore Eyes, Dyspepsia, White Swelling, Bronchitis, Asthma and Phthisic, Female Diseases, General Debility, Neuralgia, Fits, Gravel, Chills and Fever, Diarrhoe, &c. Having travelled extensively for a few years past, he has practiced in different States, from whence he has great recommendations.

[Page 92]N. B.—Having successfully treated many cases of the Cholera, in 1832-'33, as also during the last few years,—he confidentially offers his services, and recommends his Medicines to the suffering. I am happy to say that I am proving myself to be a Physician, as well as a Musician.

Certificates from persons cured by Dr. Okah Tubbee.

New Bedford, Mass., March 15, 1849.

At this time, when so many nostrums are being thrust upon the public, it is a source of great relief to the afflicted, to know that there are medicines which are truly good. Among these are the medicines of Okah Tubbee; and as I have been greatly relieved, I think it to be my duty to make a public avowal, that others may also be benefitted.

For years have I suffered the excruciating pains attendant upon rheumatism, and found no relief until I tried the medicines of Dr. Tubbee.

I only used one bottle, and am entirely free from pains; and I hereby recommend it as a medicine of great efficacy in the cure of rheumatic diseases. Let the afflicted consider this and act accordingly.

HANNAH RENDRIS.

New Bedford, Mass., March 22, 1849.

This is to certify that Dr. Okah Tubbee boarded with me four weeks and six days, and during the time he practiced on several cases, and accomplished great cures; and so great was his cures that it was astonishing to the whole city. The house was thronged from 6 A. M. to 9 P. M., and he has in his possession several certificates, of which I was an eye witness to the cures that he has done; and further than all that, I can say that he has done great cures for me and my family. Language cannot express the credit that he deserves; but I would recommend all to apply to him for remedy, as he can cure their disease let it be what it may. This I say from my heart and in the fear of God.

ELIPHALET ROBBINS.

New Bedford, Mass., March 20, 1849.

Dr. Tubbee—Sir:—I have been very agreeably surprised at the wonderful works you have done for me—both healed me soul and body. I have been sick for the last 22 months, and the doctors all told me that I had the liver complaint, but Dr. Snell and Mrs. Davis the magnetizing doctor woman could not help me. This medicine helped me, and in eight days from the time I first took it I am healed of all my complaints. Please call, in God's name, and faith believing.

I am yours, respectfully,

JOSEPH R. GARDINER, Passamaquady Tribe of Indians.

New Bedford, Mass, March 22, 1849.

Dr. Tubbee—Sir:—I embrace the present opportunity to render to you the tribute due to your skill, and also my grateful acknowledgements for the beneficial effects of your medical treatment in my family. My daughter, about six years of age, had for the last four months been afflicted with a general debility of the system, and an utter prostration of the functions of the bowels, which were much bloated. All the time we had the best medical aid we could procure, but to no purpose. She grew weaker and worse until we began with your medicines, and in little more than one week she was dressed and about the house, as this she had not done for over three months. She is now in a fair way to a perfect cure. He has also treated other cases of a more complicated nature in this city with equal skill and success. I reside at 18 Cappin-street, and will at any time cheerfully accord my testimony to his medical skill.

SAMUEL W. HAYES.

[Page 93]New Bedford, Mass., March, 1849.

To Mr. Tubbee;—This is to certify that it is with feelings of the deepest gratitude that I subscribe myself among the many that are indebted to you for the restoration of my health, which I know was fast declining. I was troubled greatly with liver complaint, dyspepsia, and which with several other complaints caused a general debility and weakness of the system. Having consulted eminent physicians, I was finally pronounced incurable. Hearing of Dr. Tubbee who performed great cures, I applied to him, and after taking his medicine for four days, I found relief, and in two weeks I felt like a new being. I therefore recommend all persons who are afflicted in any way to apply to Dr. Tubbee, who will not only relieve but cure them of all their complaints, that any human being can cure under God. Any one doubting this can call on

RHODA BERRY, 109 William-st.

New Bedford, Mass., March 16, 1849.

This is to certify that I have been afflicted for twelve months, and during that time I have had Dr. Bartlett to attend me for two months, and found no relief; and then I had Dr. Whitridge, and he said that I could not be raised; and then I applied to Dr. Gordon, and he also said that I could not survive many days. I was deprived of sleeping, and was swollen so that I could not get my clothes on. At length I applied to Dr. Tubbee, and in one night I found great relief; the swelling in my legs had gone down one third, and by taking his medicine for sixteen days, I have still great relief; the swelling has all gone out of my limbs, and I can sleep very well at night, and I can say that I feel almost as well as I ever did, except being very weak; and I recommend him to all who may be afflicted.

DAVID SAUNDERS.

Witnesses, Alia Harris, (Indian woman)
John L. Jackson.

New Bedford, Mass., March, 1849.

To Dr. Tubbee:—This is to certify that I return my sincere thanks among the many that are indebted to you for the restoration of my health, which I know was exceedingly poor. About a year ago last fall, I took a sudden cold, which settled in my limbs, and caused me to suffer greatly. I also had a cough which lasted me one year—which said cold and cough has caused my system to be greatly debilitated. I was also troubled with the complaint of the liver and kidneys. Having tried several eminent physicians, such as Mrs. Davis and Dr. B. F. Hardy of New Bedford, and Dr. Miller of Fair Haven, I found no relief. Finally, hearing of Dr. Tubbee, a most skilful physician, I applied to him, and after taking his medicine three days, found relief, and in one week, I can conscientiously say, I feel like a new man—free from all pain, cough entirely cured, and in every respect I feel well. I therefore recommend all persons afflicted with diseases of any kind to apply to Dr. Tubbee, who will not only relieve but will cure them of every complaint that human beings are subject to.

DENNIS SULLIVAN, 147 Biddle-st.

CURE OF A CANCER.

READ THIS.—Especially all those who are afflicted with Cancers, obstinate Ulcers, &c. Some years ago I suffered much pain from a white swelling. A physician succeeded in healing it, but gave me no medicine internally. This mode of treatment seemed to injure my general health. Last summer I had the measles, and they left me very much debilitated; there was a dull heavy pain about my breast and side, shoulder and arm, and at times, sharp shooting pains extending up into my neck and head. At length I could not use my arm; my neck became stiff, so much so that my head was drawn down on the diseased side; there seemed to be much inflammation about my collar bone, and extended down about one of my breasts, and near the pit of my stomach. The sore was near the collar bone, and soon spread above it. It seemed to eat daily, and [Page 94] thus increase in size. The color of the opening was black, and there seemed to be a black streak leading to the pit of the stomach; my whole breast was spotted, somewhat resembling bodies when mortification has taken place. In this situation I came to Independence; I applied to a physician; he examined the affected part, and said he did not know what it was; I asked him if he could cure me. He gave me no satisfaction, but said he would give me something for it, and handed me a box, the contents of which, he said I must apply to the affected part. Several persons who had had experience with cancers had told me it was certainly a cancer. I did not know how to proceed; I rubbed with the salve, (which proved to be nothing but mercurial ointment,) it had no good effect whatever. A friend told me of the Indian Doctor, Okah Tubbee, and advised me to go to him, which I immediately done. He at once p ounounced it a cancer, and said he should treat it as such if he prescribed for it. He commenced with it as soon as possible. I must say that the first application somewhat eased the pain and changed all appearances. In seven days the cancer on the collar bone came out by the roots, and that without pain. I took his medicine for the blood, and felt myself getting better every day. There proved to be another near the pit of my stomach, which he also brought out by the roots. It was dressed at his house every other day. Liquids injected at the collar, ran out freely at the opening near the pit of the stomach. The inflammation soon subsided; in a few days I could use my head and neck, the pains were all gone, and my countenance was again natural. And what is still more strange, in seven weeks the whole was sound and well, and has remained so until the present time. I have suffered no inconvenience whatever, but have enjoyed the best of health. I am willing to be qualified to the above. My father resides in Hickory county, Mo.

Independence, Feb. 20, 1851.

ABRAHAM CHARLTON.

I am witness to the above cure, the young man having boarded at
my house while being cured.RICHARD GOSSETT.

Missonri, Jackson Co.

Independence, Aug. 15, 1850.

This is to certify that I have been afflicted with a disease occasioned by
obstruction which is common to females, which has been of about five
years' standing, and have often been told there never was a case of the
kind removed, it having located on the skin, and which is called by some a
leprosy in the skin. Having taken medicine of Dr. Okah Tubbee, I quickly
found much relief, and in a short time found myself getting well. I have no
hesitancy in saying to the afflicted, his medicines, in whatsoever disease he
undertakes are likely to have a salutary effect.

MARTHA FRANCES CAPELL.
CHARLES CAPELL.

P. S. The above named patient was at my house during the time she
was taking O. T.'s medicine, and professed to be much relieved before she left. She also had the measles badly at the same time, and a
relapse after getting nearly well, and a violent relaxation of the bowels, attended with vomiting and cramping, of which she was relieved
in a few minutes by Dr. Tubbee's medicine.JAMES FAGG.

Independence, Feb. 9, 1851.

This is to certify that I was laboring under a deep-seated consumption last
spring and summer, and I employed several good physicians residing in

this place, (for whose attention I am thankful) yet they could not reach my case. It seemed, indeed, hopeless: I had tried all remedies within my reach, and had given up all hopes of recovery, when I heard of Okah Tubbee, the Indian Doctor. As the last resort, I applied to him. He came to me in the morning, and succeeded in breaking a tubercle in my lungs before night, from which there was a [Page 95] great discharge of the foulest matter. My symptoms were of a complicated nature; the dropsy and several other diseases were working on me at the same time. For four months I was insane, so much so that I did not know the members of my own family—this part of my complaint grew worse until I had hard fits. My life was despaired of by my husband and family, and all my friends; yet, by the blessing of God, through the skilful treatment of Dr. Okah Tubbee, all my symptoms were soon removed. My strength and flesh have returned, my appetite is natural; I am able to walk and ride about, visiting my friends and connexions, and can ride 25 miles a day. I feel it a duty to state the above facts, that the afflicted may be benefitted thereby. My husband (Joseph Moon) is willing at any time, to be qualified that the above statement is by no means an exaggeration of my case.

JANE MOON.

Vincennes, Ind., May 9, 1851.

The undersigned takes pleasure in recommending Dr. Okah Tubbee, with whom he is personally acquainted. He has attended several of his Musical Concerts, and can speak of them as the best he ever heard. To those who are fond of music I say go and hear him. To the afflicted—called and be healed on natural principles The Dr. is in possession of a number of certificates, from those whom he has relieved. Examine for yourselves.

Yours,

R. A. KING, M. D.

A cure of Liver Complaint of nine years standing.

Dr. Okah Tubbee, Toronto.

Sir:—It is with pleasure that I certify to the good effect of your medicine on myself. I have been troubled with a pain in my side, more or less, for the last nine years, and have tried several doctors, but to no effect; but after using your medicine about four days, last February, I was relieved of the pain, and have felt none of it since.

Yours truly,

JAMES A. CLARK,
No. 5 Agnes-street, Toronto.

August 2d, 1852.

A cure of Female Debility.

Sir:—This is to certify that I am now enjoying better health than for sometime before. For about two years my health was very poor, and it was thought by my friends that I was going into a decline; but being prevailed upon to use your medicine, they have, I believe, stopped the progress of disease, and now I feel as well as ever.

Yours with respect,

BETSEY CLEUGH,
Agnes Street, Toronto.

July 29th, 1852
Dr. Okah Tubbee,—Sir:—This is to certify that I am witness to the above cure.

JAMES A. CLARK.

A cure of Tumour in the Neck, caused by Erysipelas in the head.

Sir:—This is to certify, that by the use of your medicine for a few times, I was cured in one week of a tumour on my neck, which proceeded from Erysipelas in the head, and which confined me to my bed for nearly three weeks.

Yours truly,

MARIA CLEUGH,
Agnes Street, Toronto.

30th July, 1852.
Dr. Okah Tubbee.—Sir:—This is to certify that I am witness to the above cure.

JAMES A. CLARK.

A cure of Scrofula in the Leg.

Sir:—This is to certify that I was labouring under much disease from having a sore leg Hearing of Dr. Okah Tubbee, the Indian doctor, as a last resort I applied to him, who told me my disease, and prepared medicine for my leg. I felt greatly benefitted by the first application. I continued the use of the medicine, which cured me perfectly in three weeks. Dr. Okah Tubbee has [Page 96] benefitted many, to my knowledge. I feel it my duty to make this known to the public, not to benefit the doctor only, but that the afflicted may be relieved.

ALEXANDER JOHNSTON,
Dawn Mills, C. W.

June 29, 1852.

Cure of Hereditory Consumption.

Sir:—I feel it my duty to say to the invalid, there still is hope of relief. I have been greatly afflicted for the last six months with a disease of the chest—violent pain in the stomach and chest extending into the stomach, &c. I was thought to be sinking into a decline. I consulted the best physicians, but they did not agree as to my disease, I took their medicines, but they did me no good. I took a severe cough; my friends despaired of my life, and advised me to try Dr. Okah Tubbee's medicine. I have used it for four weeks, and am relieved of all those pains, and the cough also, and am now able to go out and see my friends, for which I feel truly thankful.

My mother died of consumption after a sickness of eleven years, and my brother died of consumption also, after a sickness of a year and a half.

MARY FIELDS,
At Mr. Donnely's, Victoria Street, Toronto.

Toronto, August 3, 1852.
Chief Okah Tubbee, No. 16 Victoria Street, Toronto:—We as members of the Committee appointed, feel much pleasure in presenting this "Silver Cup and Waiter" to you as a mark of high gratidute for your skill as a Doctor, in curing us of our several diseases, Consumption and Dyspepsia, which no other medical man was able to perform.

(Signed) JOSEPH JONES,
THOS. WHITLEY.

Toronto, 7th Sep. 1852.

From the Niagara Chronicle, Jan 8, 1852.

OKAH TUBBEE.—This celebrated personage has given two musical entertainments in this town to large audiences, which afforded general satisfaction.

By request we annex two certificates of some importance to Mr. Tubbee. Cayuga, October 10th, 1852.
The inhabitants of Cayuga were greatly pleased with the Musical Entertainment held at James H. Burch's Court House Hotel, last evening, by the justly celebrated Okah Tubbee, a Chief of the Choctaw Tribe of Indians. We leave the public to judge of his extraordinary musical talents for themselves. His address and account of his people, was truly interesting to us all.

J. H. BURCH.

The Cayuga Tribe of Indians, and several parties of the other tribes residing on Grand River, were delighted with their brother Okah Tubbee a chief from the Choctaw Tribe of Indians. They were amused and instructed by his address; and the Chiefs present at his Entertainment went forward to him and gave him their hands in token of acknowledgment, before his musical performance commenced. They recommend him to their pale face friends.

N. B. He gave universal satisfaction. I have not a word of fault-finding from the numerous parties present. There were over 100 whites present at the Entertainment.

GEORGE BUCK, Onondaga Indian Chief.
WM. HYFLYER, Cayuga Tribe Do.
TOM BILLS, Do. Do.
SAMUEL JACOBS, Chief Tuscarora Indians.
JOSEPH SAWYER, Chief of Chippewa Do.
MOSES POTIQUAOK, Chippewa Councilman.
Rev. P. JONES, Missionary, Chief Chippewa's.
Rev. Mr. CHASE, Interpreter, Chippewa Nation
ISAAC HILL, Onandaga Chief,
JOHN W. HIL, Mohawk Chief and Missionary.

Made in United States
Orlando, FL
22 March 2026

79569006R00076